AF538911

Insurgent Frontiers

essays from the troubled northeast

E.N.Rammohan

India Research Press, New Delhi

India Research Press
B-4/22, Safdarjung Enclave,
New Delhi – 110 029.
Ph.: 24694610; Fax: 24618637
bahrisons@vsnl.com
contact@indiaresearchpress.com
www.indiaresearchpress.com

E.N. Rammohan **2005** © ® India Research Press

ISBN : 81-87943-80-7

All rights reserved. No part of this publication unless used for research & documentation, may be reproduced, stored in or introduced into a retrieval system or transmitted in any form, or by any means, electronic, mechanical, photocopying, recording or otherwise, without the prior written permission of the publisher.

E.N. Rammohan
Insurgent Frontiers : essays from the troubled northeast

Cataloguing in Publication Data
Includes bibliographical references and index.
1. Insurgency 2. North East 3. India
I. Title II. Author

Printed in India at Focus Impressions, New Delhi – 110 003.

Foreword

It is truly amazing how ignorant our people are about the security problems in the Northeast- strategically the most important and sensitive part of our country. 98% borders of this region are international borders. Only 2% are with the rest of the country. Physically remote from the corridor of power, the region has not attracted much attention even from the so-called security experts who tend to take a simplistic view of things. It is important to understand the complexities of the many security problems, some of which have become even more complicated since the departure of the colonial rulers in 1947. And the neighbouring countries have not always been helpful. As a matter of fact, some of them are fishing in troubled waters and are not averse to actively encouraging secessionist movements in this trouble-torn region. It is very difficult to comprehend what is happening there, unless one lives there for a considerable period. The author is eminently suited to write on the security issues facing this region, as he has served many states in the Northeast extensively in various capacities. An Indian Police Service officer of the erstwhile Assam cadre he had handled some of the most difficult law and order situations during his police career. He handled the Assam riots in 1983, in which 3000 persons were killed, following the controversial elections as D.I.G.,Tejpur. He held the crucial post of I.G. (Operation) during "Operation Bajrang" and Operation Rhino". He retired as Director General of Border Security Force. Even after his retirement he served as my Advisor during President's rule in Manipur in 2001-02. An officer of scholarly bent of mind, he has been writing regularly in various prestigious magazines of the country on security issues. Some of these articles and papers are being brought out in a book form for convenient reading by all those who are interested in national security and the Northeast. The essays are informative and educative and make excellent reading and are valuable addition to the scant literature on insurgencies in the Northeast, especially Assam, Nagaland and Manipur.

Ved Marwah
Governor

Preface

November 1966, I went to Assam as a young officer and was fascinated by the people and geography of the area. This was when I had a chance to work and travel through all the states of the northeast. Later, while posted in some crucial appointments in the Northeast as Superintendent of Police in the Central Bureau of Investigation and later as Inspector General of the Central Reserve Police Force I travelled through the length and breadth of this marvelously beautiful land. I studied the history of the different peoples of the mysterious North East and the idea germinated of writing about the land and the peoples of this area. While posted as the Deputy Inspector General of Police Northern Range in Tezpur I encountered first hand the brutal elections of 1983. I had a chance to operate in counterinsurgency operations in Assam, Nagaland, Manipur and Tripura. All this finally crystallized into the three crucial essays in this book on Assam, Nagaland and Manipur.

Working in the Border Security Force. I could travel extensively along India's borders with Bangladesh and Myanmar – countries that have played a major role in the insurgencies in the Northeast, hence the paper on the porous borders of India with that state. During my tours in Tripura and Mizoram I came across the Chakmas, whom I felt had been treated most shabbily by both India and Bangladesh and I thought that I should highlight their story. Hence the last paper- The Damned of the Earth.

The lead paper in this group of essays from the

Northeast is about Assam, the biggest state of the northeast and the gateway to this fascinating region. It is of interest that Assam was never part of the big kingdoms that dominated the Indian subcontinent, starting from the empire of Asoka the great, the Kushans, the major Hindu kingdoms of the Guptas and the later Muslim empires of the Slave Kings and the Mughals. When I went to Assam in 1966. I was surprised to read about the Dimasa Cachari and Chutia kingdoms and of the Ahoms. They did not figure in the history textbooks that I had studied. It was much later after I had seen Assam and the other hill states of the Northeast and seen the way the people of this beautiful region had been exploited that I realized that the Northeast did not figure in the calculations of the people of the rest of the subcontinent. By this time I had chance to see all the seven states of the region and come to know the people to some extent. I developed a great affection for this area and I began to seriously study whatever I could get about this region.

Assam really came into the mainstream of the subcontinent only when the British East India Company went into the region in the 18th century. The first great damage was done to the region by the British who brought in four groups of people, the Adivasi tribals from Central and Southern India, the Bengali Muslim peasant from East Bengal, the Marwari trader from Northern and Western India and the Bengali babu from Bengal. They did this for their economic reasons. But it has been the root cause for all the problems of this region. It is not as if the Assamese people themselves are not to blame for the situation they are in today. It is the people from the mainland who have taught them all the wrong things. It is for this reason that I have started from the early history of Assam when writing about the insurgency of the United Liberation Front of Assam. There are many facets of this insurgency that are not known to the people of this country. I think that people have the right to know how their governments function. I have therefore been frank and forthright in writing about the Foreigners movement, and the brutal election of 1983 and the insurgency that followed. There has been no real study of the election of February 1983. It is necessary to make a thorough study of this election and how the bureaucracy behaved and let the people of this country know all the facts, so that such gross errors will not be committed again. No one really knows how many people died in the police firings, for the people who gathered to burn the bridges took most of their dead with them after the firing. I know that at least on two occasions Para Military forces deployed, opened fire with Light Machine guns to retrieve themselves. I do not think that we have ever had to fire in law and order situations with light machine guns anywhere else.

The article on Naga insurgency has a brief history of how the insurgency started and the Naga Underground fought the Indian Army and finally signed the peace agreement with the Government of India in 1975. It is the second part that traces the activities of the Nationalist Socialist Council of Nagaland, where I have written some developments in the context of Manipur that I feel should be known to the people at large. The large-scale extortions that have continued despite the presence of the Cease-fire Monitoring group are an open scandal. The common people of Nagaland and Manipur have been suffering this for the last two decades. Crores of Rupees of development money has been siphoned off by contractors and traders form the mainland and the people of Nagaland and Manipur are continuing to live in miserable conditions. It is only a small class of Politicians and bureaucrats who have benefited, and of course so have the insurgents whose leaders live in Amsterdam, Bangkok and Manila.

The paper on Manipur is written from first hand knowledge as I had the chance of operating in Manipur first as Superintendent of Police Central Bureau of Investigation, Shillong in 1979, then as Director General of Border Security Force, when we were asked to open four Subdivisions of Churachandpur District which were under the control of insurgent groups in 2000 and then finally as Advisor to the Governor of Manipur in 2001-2002. I think it is not too difficult to bring the situation under control in Manipur. You only need the Central Government to back you with men and material and a dedicated band of officers, Civil and Police. This can be done with the Politicians in the chair. I firmly believe that the civil administration is the key to tackle any insurgency. The Civil effort and the Police effort have to go side by side. President Magsaysay did this in the Huk insurgency, where he defeated the insurgents by cleaning the administration and removing the cause of the insurgents. If this can be done in the Philippines it can be done in Manipur.

The fourth paper on the Bangladesh border is again written from first hand knowledge. As Inspector General Operations and later as Director General Border Security Force, I have seen the borders of Bangladesh in West Bengal, Assam Meghalaya and Tripura quite closely. I have also had the chance to visit Bangladesh. It is of interest that in the last two years the Hindus and the Christians and the Buddhists have been targeted in Bangladesh. In 1977, there were 60 lakh Hindus in Bangladesh. Today there are probably only less than 10 lakhs, and the figure is diminishing every day. The Bangladesh Government does not publish the figures of Hindus in their Census reports. Despite all the warnings, the Central Government has never given the same importance to the Eastern Borders as they gave to the Western borders. The latest information from Bangladesh is that the fundamentalist forces have begun to attack the Sufi shrines there!

The last paper on the Chakmas is almost like a dirge for them. I have known the Chakmas in Tripura and in Mizoram and I have met them in Rangamati, Kaptai Chittagong and Cox's Bazaar. The way the Bangladesh Government has treated them has put them on the fast track to extinction. In 1964, when the then Pakistan government was constructing the Kaptai dam over the Karnaphuli river, the Government of India had agreed to rehabilitate about 30,000 Chakmas from Kaptai in India. They were brought and resettled in Arunachal Pradesh. Today they have still not been given citizenship, while lakhs of illegal immigrants from East Pakistan and Bangladesh who have come into India after that have got citizenship!

Content

1. Assam, the Foreigners' Agitation and the United Liberation Front of Assam 1

2. The Damned of the Earth 73

3. Porous Borders, Perfidious Neighbours-Security Threat from Bangladesh 83

4. The Naga Insurgency 113

5. Blue Print for Counter-Insurgency in Manipur 153

6. Index 179

Assam, the Foreigners' Agitation and the United Liberation Front of Assam

History

Assam, as it is today, was formed when many millions of years ago, Gondwana land, a part of the Antarctic landmass, which had broken off, drifted north-westwards and collided with the Asian continent. At that time a vast ocean extended from the Atlantic, through Europe and Asia, the Tethys Sea. The force of the collision was so great that a massive chain of mountain ranges buckled up from the bowels of the Earth—the Great Himalayan Range, the Karakoram and the Hindu Kush. The Tethys Sea drained out westwards; leaving behind, the Caspian Sea and the Dead Sea, salt water lakes as remnants on its retreating path. Marine fossils found all along the Himalayan range testify to the powerful forces that raised the floor of the Tethys Sea, more than five miles above sea level. The Mansarovar Lake that formed between the ranges of the Himalayas, found its outlet in two directions, the Indus to the west and the Tsang Po to the east. After traversing several hundred kilometres to the east, the Tsang Po found a gap in the mountains and turned south through a gorge at Geling, and then turning south westwards, carved out a wide valley, which became in course of time one of the most fertile places on the face of the Earth, the Brahmaputra valley. This valley is unique, because it is fed by a large number of rivers flowing into it from the north and the south. As the Earth evolved, climatically a system of annual precipitation developed, the monsoons. Taking birth in the Indian Ocean and the Arabian Sea, the south west monsoon drenches the Indian subcontinent once a year. The peculiar angle of the Brahmaputra valley serves as a funnel in the path of the advancing monsoon. As a result, this valley begins to get rain from March itself, while in the rest of India, the monsoon starts only in June. Cherrapunji and Mawsynram situated on the reverse slopes of the southern range of the Brahmaputra valley are the rainiest places in the world.

As *Homo sapiens* evolved, it was natural that this fertile valley would attract settlements. The first settlers in the valley were Tibeto-Burman tribes who migrated from Tibet and China, south and west and occupied the valley. Earlier, a Mon Khmer tribe who probably came from the south and east had settled in what is now the Jaintia Hills. Theirs is also one of the earliest kingdoms of this region. The Tibeto-Burman tribes who settled in the Brahmaputra valley were the Boros, Sonowal, Thengal and the Mech, all known as the Cacharis. A closely related group was the Chutias. They probably have an admixture of Shan blood. Other related groups are the Rabhas and the Rajbongshis, who probably have an admixture of Dravidian blood. The caste Hindus who had populated the Gangetic valley migrated into the Brahmaputra valley long after the Tibeto-Burman tribes had settled and evolved a culture and religion of their own. There is no historical evidence of when the Aryans or Dravidians migrated into the Brahmaputra valley, but there is evidence of a Kshatriya prince ruling from Kamarupa near the present Gauhati in the 4th century A.D. Pushyavarman ruled from Kamarupa and was succeeded by a line of kings well into the 5th century A.D.[1] Bhaskaravarman, the last in this line of kings was an ally of Harshavardhan and had visited Kanauj along with Hieuen Tsang, the Chinese traveller. There is no record of when the Boros and related tribes migrated into the Brahmaputra valley, or when the first migrations of the Aryans and Dravidians from the Gangetic valley into the Brahmaputra valley took place. We can only presume from the records of copper plates and coins recorded in the 4th century A.D. by the Kshatriya king Pushyavarman that the different Kachari tribes, and their related tribes like the Chutiyas, Morans, Rabhas, and the Koch Rajbongshis, were the earliest migrants and had been well settled before the migrations of the Aryans and Dravidians from the Gangetic valley took place. There is no record of any battles between the earlier tribal settlers and the later Aryan and Dravidian migrants. Presumably the caste Hindu migrants established themselves without any serious opposition from the earlier tribal settlers.

The first record of a Kachari kingdom was that of the Dimasa Kachari who established their capital at Dimapur and ruled an area from the Brahmaputra to the Dhansiri and from the Dikhow to the Kolong in the 13th century A.D. To the west was the Hindu kingdom of Kamtapur. The Chutiyas also established their kingdom with the Capital at Sadiya, in the 12th century A.D. At about this period, the Slave Kings were ruling in Delhi. In 1206 A.D. Mohammed Ibn Bukhtiyar invaded Kamrup but was defeated by its ruler King Prithu. The Muslim Generals did not give up and attacked repeatedly. King Prithu was defeated and killed by Nasiruddin, the son of Iltutmish. In the next round the Muslim army was defeated and they retreated. During their incursions a number of Assamese caste Hindus converted to Islam. These were the Assamese Muslims. Interestingly virtually no tribals were converted to Islam, though there is evidence of many tribals recruited to fight in the Muslim army. The Assamese Muslims seldom wear the purdah, and they also do not marry more than one wife. Assamese Muslims are mainly found in Nalbari and Mangaldoi districts with a scattering in other districts—Lakhimpur, Sibsagar, and Nowgong. There have been virtually no communal incidents between Assamese Muslims and the Assamese Hindus over the centuries. During their sojourn the Generals of the Slave Kings built a Mosque at Hajo in Lower Assam, which is called Pua Mecca or small Mecca, and it is even today a pilgrimage site for both Assamese Muslims and Hindus.

It was during the period when the Muslim army was routed that a Shan Prince, Sukapha with his army entered the Brahmaputra valley from the east across the Patkai range and established his kingdom near present day Nazira. To the north and east of his kingdom, the Chutiyas ruled with their capital at Sadiya, and to the west, the Dimasa Cachari ruled their kingdom from their capital at Dimapur. After the Ahoms established themselves, they did not clash with the Dimasa Cacharis for 200 years. Attacks by the Ahom kings Suhenpha and Suhenmung in the late 15th century did not succeed. It was in 1531 that the Ahom king Suhunginung defeated the Dimasa king Kungkhara.[2] The Dimasa went up into the North Cachar Hills and established their Capital at Maibong. Thenceforth they did not enter the Brahmaputra valley.

The British East India Company, after establishing itself in Calcutta had extended its operations eastwards to East

Bengal and to Cachar and then to Manipur by the 18th century. They first entered Assam in 1739 as visitors to Sib Singh, the Ahom ruler. By 1792 the British had considerable troops in upper Assam, mainly used in forays into Naga areas to punish them for raids conducted by Nagas into the plains areas. The Nagas were only objecting to the British Tea Planters trying to establish Tea Gardens in what they felt were their tribal lands. Very soon the Ahoms had been reduced to puppets. At this time palace intrigues in Manipur led to one of the princes asking for help from their traditional enemy, the Burmese king. By chance this was the time when the Burmese were particularly powerful, and they advanced into Manipur. At this juncture, one of the viceroys of the Ahom rulers, asked the Burmese for help. They promptly responded and defeating the Ahom king, laid waste the Upper Assam lands, which then comprised the Ahom kingdom. The Ahom King and his courtiers fled to the west and beseeched the British, who by then had control of Bengal and Cachar, to help them. The British alarmed at the threat to their Cachar frontier, by the Burmese promptly organised troops to be dispatched to Cachar and Gauhati. The Burmese were defeated and retreated to Manipur. There the British Governor, David Scott, had selected Gambhir Singh to drive back the Burmese. Gambhir Singh, a redoubtable General, drove back the Burmese all the way to the Kubo valley. The British then signed a treaty at Yandaboo in 1826.

In the process they annexed upper Assam to their dominion, signifying the end of the Ahom rule. At first the British were not too happy with the Upper Assam areas, for the revenue was more in lower Assam. Soon, however, the whole situation changed with the discovery of tea bushes growing wild in Upper Assam. The Government formed a Tea Committee and the first experimental tea garden was set up in 1836. Rules were amended to make wastelands available to the Tea Planters to set up tea gardens. By 1870 about 0.7 million acres of land had come under tea cultivation. With the advent of the British, the history of Assam was to change. The Burmese had laid waste the whole of Upper Assam. They had been cruel and killed thousands of innocent people. The Ahom rulers and the common people had looked for succour to the British. At first they did get this. After the dark spell of the civil wars and the unheard of cruelty of the Burmese invaders, British rule brought peace and stability to their lives.[3] Maniram Dewan, who later revolted against the British, and was hanged in 1858, had initially wished the British "uninterrupted and undiminished sovereignty for thousands of years."[4] The Assamese had not realised that the British were in India for commerce, and their attitude would change when it came to their commercial objectives.

The most striking thing about the land the British had acquired was the absence of human settlements in large parts of Assam. Between 1837 and 1851, Major John Butler of the 55th Regiment of the Bengal Native Infantry travelled widely through Assam. His is one of the early European accounts of Assam. He wrote, "In the thirty miles from Mohundijua and Dheemapoor not a vestige of any habitation or a human being could be found."[5] A number of factors now combined to start a wave of migration into Assam. The first was the requirement of labour to work in the tea gardens being set up. Back in England the fact of tea gardens being set up had set off an economic flurry in the stock market, on an even larger scale than the South Sea Bubble. The Assamese people were not willing to work in the tea gardens. The reason was not that the people were lazy, but that they had plenty of land for cultivation, and what they grew was more than sufficient for their consumption. The British had to look elsewhere for labour. There was surplus labour among the Adivasi tribals of Chota Nagpur, Bihar, and Madhya Pradesh. The British scouted even beyond these states and got Adivasi tribes from Madras province to come to Assam. They were brought by train and steamer and kept in transit sheds at Paltan Bazaar in Gauhati, before being taken to the tea gardens in Upper Assam. Once these Adivasi tribes were settled in their gardens the garden managers found that there was a problem of providing rice to the labour. The Assamese peasant was not prepared to produce more rice than they required for themselves. The British had come from Bengal to Sylhet and crossing the Khasi Hills come down to Assam. They had extensive knowledge of the East Bengal Muslim peasant. He was a demon for cultivation of paddy, jute, and vegetables. There was already overcrowding in all the East Bengal districts of Mymensingh, Rangpur, Sylhet, and land hungry peasants had nowhere to go. The British decided to open up Assam for migration of these land hungry peasants. While the Adivasi tribes had moved into Assam from the middle of the 19th century, the East Bengali Muslim started migrating from the first decade of the 20th century.

The third group of people the British brought was the Marwari trader. The East India Company officials had come across this middleman in Calcutta and were impressed with his smooth and obsequious way of operating. Incidentally, when the caste Hindus migrated into the Assam valley in the first centuries of the millennium, curiously, the Vaisyas or the trading caste did not migrate. The tribal population of Assam of that time, the Boros, Mech, Rajbongshis, Chutias, Lalungs, Moran, and the Mishings, did not know the meaning of trade. They lived by barter. In fact the caste Hindu who came from the Gangetic valley to Assam took to the barter economy from the tribals. Probably the caste Hindu of Assam is unique in that he got tribalised, incorporating several tribal words into his language and adopting a number of tribal customs and practices. The Tea Garden managers wanted middlemen in their gardens to open shops for groceries and cater to the Adivasi tribal labour. Remembering the ubiquitous Marwari trader from Bengal, he called for them and they came. To this day each tea garden has a Marwari shop that caters to the need of the labour, and even advances the wages of the labour on Bank holidays. The Marwari then found a vacuum and diversified into all the towns and villages opening shops and acting as middlemen in all trading activities. Besides tea, oil was discovered in Upper Assam and this industry attracted technical personnel and labour too, all of whom came from outside Assam

The fourth group whom the British brought was the Bengali babu. Assam did not have the requisite educated personnel to take over the clerical work in the Gardens and in the oil industry. The few educated available Assamese were taken but the majority of jobs went to outsiders, mainly Bengalis. The Assamese elite resented this invasion of the Bengali babus and their ubiquitous employment. The competition for jobs between the Assamese middle class and the Bengalis began here and was the main cause for the bitterness between the two communities. The European Planter lobby played an influential role in the Province's politics, and the Assamese intelligentsia was marginalised. This was not only due to the British preference for Bengali officials and clerks to man the Bureaucracy, but also because of the demographic changes that were taking place. By the year 1901, according to Guha, non-indigenous elements came to constitute at least a quarter of the population of Assam.[6] It was in this background that the Assamese students in Calcutta founded an Assamiya Basha Unnati Sadhani Sabha in 1888. They also brought out a journal, *Jonaki*. A virtual renaissance of Assamese literature resulted. There were also many articles bemoaning the conditions in Assam. In a paper reflecting on the state of the economy of Assam, Kamalakanta Bhattacharya wrote that the Assamese should constitute an independent self-reliant nation.[7] He warned that with the development of communications, foreigners would pour in to occupy the fertile soil of Assam, and its identity would be jeopardised. This was the first expression of the idea of a Swadhin Assam, by its intelligentsia.

The British administration had initiated a colonisation scheme to bring the land-hungry peasants of East Bengal to the Brahmaputra valley. This had led to such a vast migration, that the government introduced a line system in land holdings in 1920 to protect the land rights of the indigenous peoples. In just six years from 1930 to 1936, 59 grazing forest and village reserves were thrown open in Nowgong district under the colonisation scheme. The first wave of migration of the East Bengali Muslim peasantry into the Brahmaputra valley took place in the first years of the

20th century. Within 30 years they had made a dent in the demography of Assam. C. S. Mullen, the Census Commissioner of Assam, wrote prophetically in the census report of Assam of 1931, "Whither there is vacant land, thither goes the Mymensinghia. Without fuss, without tumult, without undue trouble, a population amounting to about half a million has transplanted itself from Bengal to Assam during the last 25 years. A time will come when Sibsagar district will remain the only district that the Assamese can call their own." It is in this background that the writings of a leading Assamese intellectual are of interest. Ambikagiri Roychoudhary, though a leading Congressman, gradually grew disillusioned and through the Asomiya Samrakhini Sabha, he wrote to Nehru in 1937 that, if the central Congress leadership did not view their fears regarding the Bengali Muslim influx seriously, then Assam should secede from India. After 1947, when the Congress Government in Assam failed to stop infiltration from the newly created East Pakistan, Roychoudhary started espousing the cause of an independent Assam through his Jatiya Mahasabha. At a meeting held on January 1, 1948, the Jatiya Mahasabha declared, "Assam should come out of the Indian Union and become an independent country like Burma.[8]" Yet another intellectual who spoke of an independent Assam was, Jnananath Bora. He spoke of the historical background of Assam and pointed out that the ancient kingdom of Kamarupa from the 4th to the 7th century remained a Hindu kingdom without being a part of any empire of Delhi. But for the British incorporating Assam as part of their empire, there was no basis for Assam being part of India.[9] A feeling of separateness gradually grew in Assam among the intellectuals through the 1930s and 1940s.

Alienation

Two factors led to a feeling that Assam was getting step-brotherly treatment. These were the way the Central Congress leadership treated the Assamese Congress leaders in the run up to partition, and the authoritarian attitude of India's first Prime Minister and Home Minister immediately after partition, on the issue of refugees from East Pakistan. Notwithstanding the fact that the Assamese took part with fervour in the Quit India movement in 1942, when scores of people were killed in police firing, they felt very badly let down when they found the central leadership of both Nehru and Patel expressing unhappiness at Assamese refusal to accept the Grouping Plan of the Cabinet Mission placing Assam along with Bengal. Initially both Nehru and Patel had advised Assam to oppose the grouping. Later Nehru expressed his unhappiness at the wording of the Assam Assembly's resolution opposing the grouping. The feeling that the Assamese leadership got was that for the good of India Assam could be sacrificed. In fact, Nehru and Patel said as much. Ultimately it was the opposition of Assam that led to the dropping of the Cabinet Mission's proposal. After partition, there was continual migration of Hindu refugees from East Pakistan into Assam. When Gopinath Bordoloi, the Chief Minister, objected to settling more refugees after 3 lakhs of them were settled in Assam, Nehru expressed his unhappiness and even threatened to reduce financial aid to Assam. The seeds of distrust between Assam and the Centre sown during this period were to grow further in the 1960s and the 70s. By 1961 the flow of Hindu refugees into Assam had reached a figure of 6 lakhs and 28 thousand.[10] In 1957, the Centre decided to construct an oil refinery at Barauni in Bihar to refine crude extracted in Upper Assam, which was to be taken by a 700-kilometre long pipeline. The indignation of the Assamese people simmered in an agitation that was the first of its kind after independence. All the political parties took part in the agitation coordinated by a Sangram Parishad. The obviously lame excuse given by the Centre that the siting of the 3.3 million ton refinery at Barauni was for defence reasons like salt in Assam's wound. If the refinery could not be protected in Assam, how could the oilfields in Upper Assam and the 700-kilometre pipeline be protected? The ultimate concession of a 0.65 million-ton refinery at Noonmati near Gauhati only confirmed the fact that Assam was getting step-brotherly treatment from the cow belt of India. The feeling that Assam would not get justice from Delhi was growing. Then came the debacle of the Chinese invasion, with the rout of the Indian Army at Tawang and the virtual decimation of a full Division. The old British district of Tezpur was ordered to be evacuated, when Nehru made a "farewell" speech to the Assamese people on All India Radio that his heart went out to them. This deeply hurt the Assamese sentiment. Working as a junior officer in the districts of Assam, I heard this being discussed by innumerable cultured Assamese families throughout the valley for many years.

Following the Sino-Indian war, the 1960s were difficult years for Assam, with shortages of rice and agitations throughout the valley. Assam was not a deficit state for rice and the only reason for the shortages were because of hoardings by the Marwaris, who had exclusive control of all trade in essential commodities, and extensive smuggling of rice to East Pakistan. I still remember, that Hojai, which was the rice bowl of Assam, had 0 per cent collection of levy rice, while North Lakhimpur, constantly under floods had a 100 per cent figure for the same. Obviously the rice from Hojai was being smuggled to East Pakistan, while in far-flung North Lakhimpur; there was no scope to take out the rice. The complete domination of all economic activities by the Marwaris finally conflagrated into a violent agitation against this community at Gauhati on the Republic Day in 1968. The rioters were all students of Gauhati, organised as a loose organisation called the Lachit Sena. The police conveniently looked the other way during the rioting. It was interesting that while property worth crores was looted and burnt, no one was injured. The trouble started immediately after the Republic Day parade at the Judges field in Gauhati. It was obviously planned well ahead, an expression of dissatisfaction and general frustration at the steadily deteriorating conditions in Assam. Interestingly, the Lachit Sena was never heard of again. The Centre was, however, not listening. There were rumours that another refinery would be constructed outside Assam. The Assamese led by the students and the left parties mounted a massive agitation for a second refinery for Assam in 1969. The state administration was paralysed for a fortnight as thousands of students from all over Assam courted arrest before the state and central government offices. The slogan was "Tez diun, Tel ne diun." We will give blood, but not oil. The Centre agreed to construct the second refinery at Bongaigaon. Once again the lesson that went home was that the Centre considered Assam as a colony, and was continuing to exploit it, like the colonising British had done. These were the heady days of the Naxalite movement in West Bengal. The Naxalite leaders seeing the growing frustration of the youth in Assam and their rising anti-India feelings moved their operation eastwards and opened cells in the Lower Assam districts. It is interesting that the mentor of the first anti-national underground group that was formed in Assam, in Pithakhowa village of Tezpur district in 1982, the Assam Peoples Liberation Army (A.P.L.A.) was a Naxalite, a schoolteacher of Bihaguri School. As Deputy Inspector General of Police, Northern Range, Tezpur in 1982-84, I had interrogated the principal players in this transaction, when they were arrested.

Two issues had by now crystallised in Assam, the continually deteriorating economic situation of the State and the continuing illegal migration from East Pakistan. The annual economic growth rate of Assam for the period 1970-80 was a mere 0.4 per cent compared to the all India average of 1.43 per cent for the same period. The number of the unemployed during this period increased by 270 per cent, while that of the uneducated unemployed was 343 per cent. The job sector in the State Government was stagnant. It was well known that the Central Government and its Public Sector were unsympathetic to local recruits. The employment review committee of the Assam Legislative Assembly said as much in its report.[11] There was a reason for this. During the British rule, virtually all Central Government departments had their eastern region H.Q.s located at Calcutta. This continued well after independence. All recruitment for subordinate posts was naturally made from there, and the local applicants of the Northeastern states were seldom successful in the interviews. Local candidates were also not preferred by the Central Public Sector organisations. The percentage of Assamese employees in the subordinate ranks in all Central Government offices and Public Sector Undertakings never exceeded 30 per cent, while in other states local employees had more than 90 per cent representation.

In the 1970s it began to dawn on the Assamese people that the three main industries of the State—Tea, Oil, and Coal were not having any impact on the economy of Assam. The 756 tea gardens in Assam produced 55 per cent of the country's tea and earned foreign exchange of Rs. 500 crores. Assam however got only Rs. 22 crores as sales tax, while West Bengal got Rs. 42 crores, for the year 1980. This was because many of the tea companies had their H.Q.s in Calcutta. In the case of plywood, the state got just 35 lakhs, while the Centre got Rs. 80 crores, for the same year.[12] The production of crude from the oil fields of Upper Assam had gone up from 0.1 million in 1962 to 3.5 million tonnes per year in the 1970s due to the discovery of new oilfields. The royalty paid to Assam in 1979 was a mere Rs. 42 per tonne. The centre refused to raise the state's share of royalty, despite pleas from the state. The feeling that the Centre was only exploiting the state's natural resources began to gain increasing credence among the Assamese people as the 1970s progressed.

The second issue of illegal migration from East Pakistan and later after its liberation, Bangladesh, was a complex problem. The British had officially encouraged migration of Bengali Muslim peasants from East Bengal to the Brahmaputra valley districts of Kamrup, Nowgong, Darrang and Goalpara in the first decade of the 20th century as a policy, to fill up large tracts of vacant land in these districts and to increase the production of paddy. As mentioned earlier, the result of this policy was a virtual inundation of the lower Assam valley districts by Bengali Muslims from East Bengal. C.S.Mullen, the Census Commissioner had sounded the first warning in 1931. Even before that by 1920, the pressure to occupy vacant lands by the East Bengali Muslims was so intense that the Assamese people represented to the British Government to restrict further occupation of grazing reserves. The government realising the gravity of the problem introduced the line system that designated the area in each district that could be settled by the immigrant Muslims from East Bengal. The immigrant Muslim leaders vehemently objected to this. Despite the government's efforts the geography of Assam and the venality of its petty bureaucrats, helped thousands of immigrant Muslim peasants to settle outside the demarcated lands and even in the tribal blocks, where land could not be transferred to a non-tribal Assamese let alone an immigrant from outside the state. The fourth Saadullah Ministry, August 1942 to March 1945, dereserved grazing reserves in Kamrup, Nowgong and Darrang districts for settling East Bengali Muslim peasants. Lord Wavell, the Viceroy, described the new settlements as "Grow more Muslims" rather than "Grow more food."

The Brahmaputra and its tributaries have land on either bank that is low-lying, called 'dao matti' in Assamese. This is inundated during the rainy season, but become sand banks during the dry season. In the Brahmaputra and in the larger of its tributaries, large sand banks are also exposed in midstream during the dry season. These are called chapories or chars. The soil of the chapories and the Dao matti areas is extremely fertile and paddy, sesame and mustard are grown with very little effort. Since the land of the chapories and the dao matti is not permanent, and changes its configuration with each season, it cannot be surveyed. It is non-cadastral land, and no deeds can be prepared for this land. The Bengali Muslim immigrant from East Bengal settled on these chars and chapories all along the length of the Brahmaputra in the central and lower Assam districts. The Assamese peasants never cultivated the chapories, or chars, but they used to cultivate the dao matti areas along the bank of the rivers, planting sesame and mustard during the winter months. This was called Pam Khethi. When the immigrant Muslims settled on the dao matti areas along the banks of the streams and the main river, the pam Khethi of the local people was naturally disturbed. This was one of the pressure points, and in the brutal elections of 1983, there would be massive rioting on such disputed strips of land. Life on the chars and in the low-lying areas on the banks of the Brahmaputra and its tributaries was exceedingly difficult.

The rains would commence in March and continue till October. During this period there would be two or three waves of floods. The immigrant Muslims living on the chars used to construct only temporary huts for themselves. When the rains came, they would shift their poultry, goats and cattle to high ground created by piling up mud and banana plants, and sit out the floods, living in boats for a couple of days, till the flood levels went down, and they could shift to their temporary huts. Very often, the chapories would get eroded, and the homestead areas washed away. The char dwellers were prepared for such conditions. They would shift their cattle and meagre possessions to boats and move to the embankments, and live in temporary makeshift sheds, patiently waiting for the river to refashion a new chapori. Once this was formed, they would shift to it and build their temporary sheds, and commence planting paddy for the next Sali crop. It was only the hardy East Bengali Muslim peasant who could surmount such harsh conditions and survive. The Assamese peasant or even the East Bengali Hindu never ever thought of trying to live on the chars. When the line system was drawn up and no political patronage came their way after the Saadullah Ministry, the East Bengali Muslim began to move into the vacant space of the chars, and later into the low-lying lands along the banks of the Brahmaputra.

In their search for vacant lands, the corrupt petty bureaucracy of Assam also abetted the Bengali Muslim peasant. There were a host of petty officials – Revenue, Forest and Police who for a consideration helped the East Bengali peasant settle on vacant lands, getting land transferred from poor tribals in the tribal belts, recommending an application for citizenship, and allowing settlement in forest land. Their senior officers also had a role in this and there were many Extra Assistant Commissioners, Sub-Divisional Officers, Additional Deputy Commissioners, Deputy Commissioners, District Forest Officers and Superintendents of Police who helped settle the Bengali Muslim immigrants, some out of communal, and others for pecuniary considerations. During the British days, the politicians did not have a role in this nefarious business, except for the Saadullah Ministry, that encouraged Bengali Muslim migration into Assam, because of the Muslim factor. After independence, for the first ten years, the politicians did not play any role in illegal migration. During this period it was solely the Assamese bureaucrat who was involved. Through the 1950s, both the

Centre and the state were serious about detecting and deporting the illegal migrant. Despite this, illegal migration continued. It was B.N. Mallick, the Director of the Intelligence Bureau who drew the attention of the Central Government to this phenomenon of continual migration of East Pakistan Muslims into Assam, West Bengal and Tripura. As a result, a Pak Infiltration Post (P.I.P.) scheme was instituted in Assam, and related schemes of a Special Task Force were set up in West Bengal and Tripura. During the two decades after independence, the State Government was serious about detecting and deporting East Pakistan nationals. The Assamese bureaucrats were more enthusiastic about deporting the East Pakistani Hindus. During this period the corruption factor involved only the Assamese bureaucrats. It was only as the 1970s commenced that it slowly began to dawn on the politicians particularly at the Centre that the East Bengali Muslim was a safe election bet.

Henceforth, it was the politician and the increasingly spineless bureaucrats who began to chorus "Yes Sir, Yes Sir, Three bags full Sir," who carried out their bidding by settling Bengali Muslim immigrants. I was witness to this as Deputy Inspector General of Police, Northern Range, Tezpur during 1982-1983. There was a vast area of Dao Matti, low-lying land, on the north bank of the Brahmaputra in Mangaldoi Sub Division called Chawalkhowa Chapori. This consisted of a big chapori and a number of smaller chapories separated from the main bank of the river by a narrow channel called a Huti, which dried up in the dry season. This chapori was vacant till 1962, when the first illegal migrants from East Pakistan settled on it. By 1982, there were a dozen villages on this group of chapories, and the Assamese villagers on the bank of the river had long since discontinued their Pam Khethi there. There was an Assamese Muslim village Sanua, on the bank of the Brahmaputra, whose inhabitants used one of the vacant chapories of this group as a grazing reserve, kept a herd of buffaloes on this during the dry season. Milk from these buffaloes used to be taken to Gauhati by boat daily. In 1982, suddenly a group of immigrant Muslims settled on this chapori and started constructing temporary huts, and began ploughing a part of the chapori, which they fenced off. The people of Sanua went to the chapori and objected to this, telling the immigrant Muslims who had settled there, that this chapori was a grazing reserve of Sanua, meant for their milch buffaloes. The immigrants, who were probably fresh infiltrants from Bangladesh, refused to leave the chapori, and further as if to show their insouciance, killed and cut up a buffalo. The villagers of Sanua then represented to the Sub-Divisional Officer, who incidentally was an upright young officer, and who promptly inquired into the matter. Convinced on the basis of the enquiry, that it was a clear case of encroachment, he ordered eviction of the trespassers. Even as the eviction was being carried out, the Sub-Divisional Officer was getting phone calls from Gauhati to stop the eviction. This was during President's rule.

Obviously the immigrant Muslim lobby had got through to Delhi. The officer refused to act on verbal orders. He was, however, forced to withdraw the armed force deployed there and the immigrants came back to the chapori, and resettled there. When the elections were announced in January 1983, the people of Sanua went to the chapori and told the immigrant Muslim settlers there that they should not vote as they were foreigners. They refused. Starting from

January, all over Assam, the volunteers of the All Assam Students Union and the Sangram Parishad had started burning all wooden bridges to ensure that communications to the interior were cut off, so that election parties could not reach the polling booths. On February 7, 1983, big mobs from the Assamese villages on the main bank attacked the immigrant Muslim villages of Chawalkhowa chapori. The Assamese Muslims of Sanua attacked the encroachers of the chapori on which their buffalos used to be kept. When I visited the area after the elections were over to try and evacuate the survivors, the immigrant Muslims of the chaporis told me that they were surprised to see that their attackers were Muslims from Sanua. More than a hundred immigrant Muslims were killed in the attacks that night. Nearly a dozen Assamese attackers were also killed, including the brother of Joynath Sarma, a leader of the Sangram Parishad and head of the Swecha Sewak Bahini; a youth volunteer corps of the movement. One of the killed was an Assamese Muslim boy of Sanua who was one of the Assamese Muslims who attacked the illegal immigrant Bengali Muslims of Chawalkhowa Chapori. The monument erected by the All Assam Students Union in his memory stands in Sanua village. This was probably the first time that a Muslim mob attacked another Muslim mob in India. The party in power in Delhi always tried to show that the rioting in Assam was on communal lines. Religion was never an issue. The issue was land.

The Zhia Bharali was a big river that flowed into the Brahmaputra just east of Tezpur. Near its confluence with the Brahmaputra, a number of small chapories had formed. These used to be submerged during the rains and surface during the dry season. On the east bank of this river was a big Assamese village Jamuguri, whose villagers, used the small chapories that used to surface during the dry season for their Pam Khethi. At the confluence of the Zhia Bharali with the Brahmaputra was a big chapori, which had been colonised by illegal Bengali Muslim immigrants. After the small chapories near Jamuguri village surfaced in the winter of 1982, a few Bengali Muslims from the main chapori at the confluence of the Zhia Bharali and the Brahmaputra, moved upstream and settled on the chaporis near Jamuguri. Since this happened to be the Pam Khethi of the villagers of Jamuguri, they went to the island and objected to the encroachers. The illegal immigrants who had settled, refused to listen to the requests of the villagers, and built temporary shelters, and started farming. The villagers of Jamuguri then submitted petitions to the Deputy Commissioner Tezpur, who took no action on the matter, probably due to the ubiquitous telephone calls. When the agitation against the elections was announced, the villagers of Jamuguri decided to take action to evict the illegal settlers themselves. At night a selected group from the village came by boats to the small chapories and attacked the immigrant Muslims who had built temporary huts. They killed two Bengali Muslim encroachers. The others managed to escape in boats to the main chapori. The police visited the spot and registered murder cases, but could find no clue of the accused. About a month later there was a big riot as the villagers of Jamuguri, attacked the large chapori at the confluence of the Zhia Bharali and the Brahmaputra. Later when the situation was brought under control, a senior administrative officer, who was known to be communal and was also known to be close to a former Chief Minister, asked me to deploy C.R.P.F. on the two small chapories of Jamuguri and bring back the illegal immigrants who had fled after the murder of two of them by the villagers of Jamuguri. I informed the official that the chapories in question were the Pam Khethi of the people of Jamuguri, and the immigrant Muslims had illegally settled on them. How could we give police protection for illegal immigrants? The official and his political mentor were obviously unhappy, but they could do nothing about it. They did not have the courage to give me written orders.

The Foreigners' Agitation

By the late 1970s, the Assamese people began to feel that the Bengali Muslim immigrant constituting the largest vote bank in the state was fast emerging as a viable political entity. At this time the sitting member of the Mangaldoi Lok Sabha constituency died, and a by-election was to be held. When the electoral list was being revised, the Chief Election Commissioner of India expressed concern that a large section of the electorate of this constituency were foreigners. While the electoral rolls were being revised, a tribunal set up by the State Government, declared 45,000 voters of this constituency of 6 lakhs, as foreigners. At the initiative of the All Assam Students Union (A.A.S.U.) that had been recently constituted, the All Assam Gana Sangram Parishad was formed at Dibrugarh in August 1979. It consisted of several regional parties, the Assam Sahitya Sabha, the Assam Jatiyatbadi Yuba Chatra Parishad (A.J.Y.C.P.) and the A.A.S.U. It was at this point that political events took a hand. Morarji Desai's Janata Government collapsed as Charan Singh defected, and a coalition Government was formed with the Congress driving from behind. Openly a vote bank of the Congress party, the Immigrant Bengali Muslim lobby began to exert pressure on the Central Government to go easy on the revision of the electoral rolls of Mangaldoi constituency. The Chief Election Commissioner, who had originally raised the issue of foreigners in the electoral rolls of this constituency, lost his guts and humbly recanted and stated that the 1977 electoral rolls would serve for this by-election. The Government issued orders that no names will be deleted from the electoral rolls. However, by this time on the basis of the earlier orders issued by the Election Commission, 3,20,000 complaints and objections had already been filed. The Chief Election Commissioner is a Constitutional Authority, and he could have stood his ground. His humble recantation changed the course of history. The Gana Sangram Parishad started the Assam Movement. On November 6, 1979, a mass rally of students was organised by A.A.S.U. at Gauhati. Four days later the first phase of the agitation began, with students and others offering Satyagraha in the manner of the freedom struggle and courting arrest. The response was massive. Thousands of people came up for arrest every day. Naturally the jails could not accommodate so many people. The government arrived at an understanding with the volunteers. They were formally arrested and released. As the movement gained momentum, the Gana Sangram Parishad and the A.A.S.U. asked all political parties to boycott the elections.

There is no doubt whatsoever that the movement had a popular base. As a direct witness to the agitation, I can vouchsafe that such a movement had not taken place after the 1942 civil disobedience movement. From children of 10 years to old men and women—70 to 80 years old—everyone participated in the agitation. Schools and colleges stopped functioning. In fact all the students of Assam lost a year during the agitation. Such a thing had never happened in the country before. The A.A.S.U and the Sangram Parishad were asking for the detection and disenfranchisement of foreigners in accordance with the National Register of Citizens 1951. The agitation was backed by all sections of the Assamese people, urban and rural. For the Assamese this was the last fight to ensure the survival of their identity and culture.[13] Though the A.A.S.U. projected it as a national movement, there was a clear secessionist undercurrent to the movement. Two of the constituents of the agitation, the A.J.Y.C.P. and the regional party had secessionist feelings. In fact the A.J.Y.C.P. was the most interesting of the constituents of the movement. Formed in March 1978 it was to be the main feeder organisation of the future insurgent group, the United Liberation Front of Assam. (U.L.F.A.) While it shunned politics, its organising ability was excellent. One organisation that was formed by Joynath Sarma, one of the A.A.S.U., leaders was an example of the inner discipline of the movement. This volunteer body had representatives in every Assamese village and urban locality of Assam. News of an impending bandh was disseminated throughout the State before the Special Branch got wind of it. The different departments of the Government were captive to the movement. The State Police Wireless Organisation and the Central Government's Department of Telephones were also totally with the movement. The Assamese have a unique institution, the Naam Ghar, the place of worship without idols gifted by her great religious reformer Shanker Dev. Every village and urban locality has its Naam Ghar. Here the local people gather after the day's labour to sing hymns and discuss the affairs of the State. I was Deputy Inspector General of Police Northern Range at Tezpur in 1982-83 at the peak of the agitation. One evening, I had stopped by at the house of a friend and was sitting in his verandah. Opposite was a Naam Ghar. Suddenly we saw the housewives of the locality assembling in the Naam Ghar. It was rather early in the evening for people to gather in the Naam Ghar. The ladies, who had assembled in the Naam Ghar, sat down, had some discussions and then quietly dispersed. My friend then asked me if there was a bandh the following day. I had not heard of any bandh, and said so. I rang up the Inspector General Special Branch in Gauhati, who also confirmed that there was no information of a bandh the next day. I asked him to check up, as I was sure that there would be a bandh. Two hours later, I got a call from the same officer that A.A.S.U. had called for a bandh, and he asked me how I knew about this. How was I to tell him that a chance sighting of an assembly of housewives in a Naam Ghar had given me the clue?

As the movement progressed, it took various forms. There were calls for all lights to be switched off throughout Assam for an hour in the evening, for all houses to sound gongs in their houses at designated times, for the movement of oil from the refineries to be stopped. The movement also saw acts of violence from bomb blasts on the refinery pipeline to threats and intimidation. The A.A.S.U. leaders were called to Delhi and the party in power tried every blandishment to lure them to a settlement, with the Intelligence agency of the Government doing all the dirty work of holding out the carrots. The leaders of the movement to their credit remained steadfast and refused to be tempted. They did succumb later when they came to power, but that is another story. The A.A.S.U. was not asking for anything impossible. They were asking the Government to function in accordance with the Constitution and the Indian Citizenship Act. They were asking for the Government to identify people of erstwhile East Pakistan and Bangladesh, who had illegally migrated into Assam to be detected and disenfranchised. These were illegal immigrants whose settlement had been abetted very often by Assamese officialdom, but who were now being protected by political parties who had made them a vote bank. The bankrupt political leadership in Delhi was thinking only of the next day, the next election. There was no one to think of the next generation, of the nation's tomorrow. There were no statesmen in Delhi. A national tragedy was looming and the crescendo was rising.

The party in power in Delhi had decided to hold elections in Assam, and called the A.A.S.U. leaders for one last meeting to persuade them to accept 1971 as the cut off year. In 1972, after the liberation of Bangladesh, Sheikh Mujibur Rehman while signing the Indira Mujib Pact had stated that he would not take back any of the people of East Pakistan who had crossed over to India, before March 21, 1971. India's Prime Minister agreed to this, not thinking that she was legalising illegal entrants who had committed an offence under the Indian Citizenship Act. In the euphoria of the liberation of Bangladesh and the defeat of Pakistan, no one raised this issue. In fact such a decision could not have been taken even by Parliament, since it was a question of exonerating people who had committed criminal offences. The decision to make 1971 the cut off year was conditioned by the concession given to Bangladesh. In Delhi, the students did not agree, and they were all arrested at Gauhati's Borjhar airport when they returned from Delhi. The elections were announced and the movement of the largest contingent of para-military forces ever sent to any state began. Incredibly the election was to be on the basis of the 1977 electoral rolls. By now unbeknown to the government, the extremist wing of the Assam movement had crystallised into the first insurgent secessionist group, the A.P.L.A. The architect behind this group was a Naxalite theoretician; a teacher in Bihaguri High School, near Tezpur and it had its base in Dipota Bihaguri and Pithakhowa villages. With the beginning of the Assam movement, the flow of intelligence on the movement had begun to dry up. This was because the movement involved all the people of Assam. The police were holding out, but one could sense the undercurrent of sympathy. Repeated violation of curfew by thousands of people told its own tale. For those of us who had their ear to the ground, it was clear that there was going to be a blood bath if the elections were held. The classic signs of an impending insurgency were written in gigantic letters as if on a canvas across the Brahmaputra valley. I remember quoting from Sir Robert Thompson's *Defeating Communist Insurgency,* in a letter to the government, "One of the signs of an incipient insurgency is the drying up of information."

Assam has two main national highways, one on the north bank and the other on the south bank of the Brahmaputra river. There are smaller roads, leading from the two national highways roughly north and south, and further branch roads. A large number of rivers flow south from the Himalayas and northwards from the Garo, Khasi, Jaintia, Mikir, North Cachar and Naga hills. All these rivers have hundreds of tributaries and nullahs. The interior roads of Assam have hundreds of wooden bridges across the innumerable streams and nullahs. There were wooden bridges across the Bor Nadi and other big streams on the national highway. There were some wooden railway bridges on the line to Murkong Selek, the north easternmost corner of the state. The extremist wing of the Sangram Parishad had organised well. The first incidents after the announcement of the election were the burning of the innumerable wooden bridges across the hundreds of streams in the interiors. The objective was obvious. Cut off communications to the interiors, so that election parties could not move to their locations. There were peculiar incidents that clearly sent across messages. Patherighat was a small bazaar in the interior of Mangaldoi subdivision. A small patrol post of the state police was located in one room of a two-roomed primary school. A section of the Assam police battalion was sent to reinforce the post. One day the Asst Sub Inspector of the post was returning on his cycle from a visit to his parent police station Sipajhar, when he noticed smoke spiralling up as he neared his post. He speeded up and when he reached the post found it in flames. The six constables and the section of battalion personnel were sitting under a tree with their weapons and bedding and the C.G.I. sheets of the roof of the school building stacked beside them. According to the Havildar who was in charge, a crowd of about 1000 people, some as old as seventy and others as young as ten years, armed with petrol and kerosene assembled around the school and asked them to vacate. They said they did not want to commit any offence, but as the Government was not listening to their request to delete the names of foreigners, they could not allow voting to take place in the school. They had therefore no choice but to burn the school down. They asked the Havildar to remove their belongings, weapons and even the C.G.I. sheets from the roof. The Havildar and his men who had all taken positions hesitated to fire on the crowd. An old man who was the spokesperson told the battalion personnel that they could fire if they wanted, but they were more than a thousand and how many could the police party kill before they could be overpowered? The Havildar claimed that he chose discretion as the better part of valour. There were many incidents like this. In some, the police fired and dozens of people were injured and killed before the crowd dispersed. It was impossible to protect the innumerable small wooden bridges, and as each one burnt polling booths were cut off.

By now the Intelligence Agencies of the Central Government had long since ceased to give independent professional intelligence to the government and had become committed to the party in power. It is to the everlasting shame of the Central Intelligence Agencies that they did not give a true assessment of the ground situation to their political masters but with servile sycophancy toed the line of the political leaders. A senior intelligence officer had been posted to the Northeast a few weeks before the elections. He was one of the few professionals in the agency. He had not handled the Northeast before and he was horrified at what he saw and heard and said so in a report. His conclusion was that there would be a bloodbath if the elections were held. He was summoned to Gauhati and berated on the tarmac of the airfield as if he was a recruit and summarily reverted to his state after 20 years in the Agency. The message was clear. Write what the political bosses want to hear, not as per the ground situation. Committed bureaucracy was the legacy of the Emergency and regrettably has been increasingly used by all political parties, even the ones who were victims of this during the Emergency.

The extraordinary election of February 1983 was not going to be an election. It was a tussle between the Assamese people and the Central Government to see if the election could be held. In this the people were the undoubted victors, but at a terrible cost. More than 6,000 people died in the ethnic clashes and the police firing. The election was a gory farce. The party in power had split the population in two groups, the Assamese on one side and the Bengali Hindus and Immigrant Muslims on the other. The Boros were also divided on the issue. The Saraniya Boros, who were Boros who had taken "Sharan" with the Caste Hindus, were with the Assamese, while the Boros, who had remained as tribals were for the elections. The Central Intelligence Agencies had done their nefarious work well. They had been building up this divide assiduously during the run up to the elections. Political leaders of the ruling party also played a role in this, touring the immigrant Muslim and the Boro areas and instigating both the groups against the Assamese. The main fallout of the bloodbath of an election was the decision of the extremist wing of the Assam movement to take to arms. The U.L.F.A. has always held that it was raised in 1979. This was not true. The Intelligence Agencies also continued with this fiction. It was actually raised in 1983, after the brutal and horrifying election that was forced on the Assamese people. As Inspector General Operations in Assam from 1990, the commencement of Op Bajrang, till February 1993, I interrogated dozens of U.L.F.A. cadres, including several top leaders who all told me that the 1979 date was notional.

The decision to take to arms was made only after the terrible election of February 1983.

The whole State Government went on strike from February 2. It was the date fixed for the commencement of coordinated action all over the State. Neither the Central nor the State intelligence agencies had a clue to this. Mobs of five to six thousand people assembled all along the national highway from Sipajhar to Mangaldoi and tried to set fire to the two wooden bridges on this road. They also assembled on the road from Mangaldoi to Kalaigaon and Tangla and set fire to all the wooden bridges en route. A mob of five thousand people even tried to set fire to a concrete bridge near Mangaldoi. The fury of the mob was such that in places armed police from the District simply fled from the scene. The C.R.P.F. led by its officers and the Superintendent of Police Tezpur opened fire at more than a dozen places before the mobs dispersed. It was as if the people had developed a death wish. The day's toll was 22 killed in police firing. At least that was the figure of dead bodies collected after the mobs were dispersed. It was not known how many dead bodies were carried away, by the mobs. The national highway to Tezpur was open, but the road to Kalaigaon and Tangla was cut off. From the next day the whole of Assam was under a natural curfew. All vehicles ceased plying, all State Government offices were closed, and all shops were closed. A deathly silence descended on the land. It was eerie driving on the road. The roads were deserted. No human being could be seen on the road. But you had the uncanny feeling that eyes were watching you as you drove by. The telephone exchanges were taken over by the Army Signals, and the water supply by the M.E.S. Only the hospitals functioned. Throughout the day reports came in of bridges going up in flames, of all buildings designated as polling booths being set on fire. Reports of ethnic clashes did not appear immediately, because they took place in the interiors where all communications had been cut off. I do not think such a situation has been seen by any state in the country before or after. This self imposed curfew lasted for 19 days. The polling was on February 7, 14 and 21, 1983.

Assamese mobs attacked Chawalkhowa chapori on February 7. In the clashes over a hundred immigrant Muslims were killed. North of Mangaldoi was a village called Khoirabari. Here in a cluster of villages lived a couple of hundred Bengali Hindus, who had been settled here in the lands vacated by Bengali Muslims, who had gone to East Pakistan in 1947. For years the Assamese Hindu villages around them had been resentfully looking at them. After the communications to Khoirabari were cut off, the Assamese of the neighbouring villages surrounded them and attacked at night. More than a hundred Bengali Hindus were killed. The rest took shelter in the Khoirabari railway station. The first phase of polling held on the February 7 in Mangaldoi subdivision and in other parts of Assam was a complete farce. In the exclusive Immigrant Muslim and Boro areas, near the national highway, where there were communications, there was substantial voting. In the exclusive Assamese areas not a single vote was cast. Here the polling booths each had a platoon of C.R.P.F., guarding the polling personnel, who incidentally had all been imported from outside the State. The polling booths in the interior were not set up, as there was no communication to them. Some of these polling booths were set up on the national highway. Naturally there was no polling in them. No election Commission worth its name would have upheld this kind of Election. Yet such was the degree of sycophancy, that with polling figures of 350, or 400 in an electorate of a lakh and with not even 10 polling booths set up correctly, candidates were declared elected.

North Lakhimpur was to have polling in the second phase on the February 14. While the attention was on Mangaldoi, the villagers of the area from Jamuguri to North Lakhimpur were busy creating roadblocks on the national highway. Along a length of 100 kilometres, more than 30 to 40 trees had been felled across the highway. Trenches had been dug across the road. We went to North Lakhimpur by helicopter. The situation in the district was chaotic. Except for one constituency, which was dominated by immigrant Muslims, the Assamese controlled the other six. All communications to the interior were cut off. It was virtually impossible to set up any polling booths in the interior. It was here that a curious incident took place. On the morning of February 11, I was in the circuit house with a senior Administrative Officer known to be close to the party in power. I was busy on the telephone getting reports of violent incidents all over the district. At that moment a former Chief Minister and active leader of the party in power at Delhi walked into the room and started talking to my colleague, who called me over and introduced me to the politician. He told me that the pressure on the police was too much and something would happen at Gohpur on February 12, that would remove the pressure on the police. I did not understand him and asked him what could happen at

Gohpur that would relieve the pressure from the police. To this he replied, "Wait and see." The telephone rang again and I took the call to listen to more incidents of violence, after which I left for the trouble spots. In the midst of all the trouble, I missed the significance of what the politician told us. Gohpur was the last big town of Darrang district, situated about 120 kilometres from Tezpur. It was completely cut off from Tezpur and from North Lakhimpur, by innumerable roadblocks. Gohpur was a predominantly Assamese area, except for the Gohpur Reserve forest on the Arunachal border, which had been encroached by Boros, who had spread out in a dozen forest villages. In the run up to the elections, the Assamese people of Gohpur had asked the Boros to boycott the elections. The Boros refused. There was already bad blood between the Boros and the Assamese because of the Boros having forcibly occupied the Gohpur Reserve Forest. The Assamese volunteers then burnt all the wooden bridges to the Boro area and no polling party could go there. Incidentally, the Assamese of Gohpur were very rough and overbearing in their behaviour. They resorted to violence easily and took up causes and fought for it tenaciously. In 1942, a young 14-year-old schoolgirl from Gohpur had carried the national flag and challenged the police who opened fire. The girl Kanakalata Barua was right in front and was killed in the firing, holding the national flag.

On February 12, a mob of about a thousand Boros from the Gohpur Reserve forest suddenly swooped down on a dozen Assamese villages between Gohpur town and the Reserve Forest area. The mob attacked the surprised villagers and set fire to their houses. The Assamese fled and took shelter in Gohpur town, where the police and C.R.P.F. were located. Sitting in North Lakhimpur, on the 12th, we could get only vague reports that some serious rioting and arson had occurred. We immediately set out for Gohpur, but could only come up to Bihupuriya because of the massive roadblocks. While waiting near Bihupuriya, trying to clear the road blocks, I suddenly remembered what the politician friend of my colleague had told me on the 11th, the day before, that some big incident would take place at Gohpur on the 12th which would take away the pressure from the police. How did the politician know on the 11th what would happen on the 12th? I suddenly realised that his party had engineered this attack. The planners had probably been misguided by their Intelligence appreciation that the Assamese would take this lying down. On the 14th, while we were busy with the polling in North Lakhimpur, a huge mob of Assamese from at least 20 odd villages stretching from Gohpur to Bihupuriya swept across the dozen odd villages of the Boros in the Gohpur Reserve Forest, killing more than 100 Boros. The hapless Boros fled across the border to Arunachal Pradesh. We came to know all this later. Immediately after the election was over, we went into the Gohpur Reserve Forest Area and along the Arunachal Border Area and talked to the Boros. Piecing together the evidence, we managed to find two Boros from Kokrajhar. On questioning, they admitted they had been sent from Kokrajhar to instigate the Boros of Gohpur Reserve Forest to attack the Assamese people of Gohpur. While we were interrogating these two Boros, a special team from the Assam Special Branch arrived and took them to Dispur. Naturally, we did not hear of this matter again.

What happened in Nellie across the Brahmaputra on

the north bank was horrifying. There were a number of immigrant Muslim villages that had come up in the tribal belt of the Lalung or Tiwa tribe near Jagi Road in Nowgong district. The settlement of these immigrant Muslims, all illegal migrants was probably done by collusion of petty bureaucrats. The Tiwa were simple and were easily bought over. There were a number of incidents of Tiwa girls being enticed and kidnapped by immigrant Muslim boys. When the foreigners' agitation started, the neighbouring Tiwa and Assamese villagers went to the immigrant Muslim villagers and asked them not to vote. They did not agree. From Jagi road the Northeast Frontier Railway line extended southeastwards. On this axis were two Assamese villages, Jamunamukh and Khampur. These were the last Assamese villages of Nowgong district. Beyond this was a solid immigrant Muslim belt all the way to Hojai, a subdivisional town. Alternatively, if you came from Nowgong to Hojai, Doboka was the watershed where the immigrant Muslim area began, and the Assamese villages ended. The C.R.P.F. had been deployed in an arc from Doboka via Khampur to Jamunamukh along the interface between the Assamese and the immigrant Muslim villages, basically to prevent any serious ethnic clashes from breaking out. The C.R.P.F. Commandant of the battalion deployed had worked with me earlier, and he told me what had happened. The Assamese villagers hated the C.R.P.F. because they did not hesitate to beat up the Assamese protesters during the foreigners' agitation. Just before the polling, the battalion deployed in the Doboka, Khampur, Jamunamukh belt received orders to withdraw and redeploy on the north bank, immediately after the polling. The tension between the Assamese villagers and the immigrant Muslims was very high. There were wild rumours that if the polling were successful, the Assamese would be taught a lesson as soon as the C.R.P.F. withdrew. Curiously, when the news spread that the C.R.P.F. was going to withdraw, the Assamese villagers ran to the C.R.P.F. camps and begged the post commanders not to withdraw. Throughout the period of the agitation, the C.R.P.F. was hated and nowhere were the same Assamese villagers, swallowing their pride and begging the post commanders not to vacate their posts. The post commanders naturally reported this to their Commandant, who informed the civil administration. The orders came back to withdraw. On this the Commandant went to each of the posts and interacted with the Assamese villagers. They were frantic and begged him holding his feet that they were sure that as soon as the C.R.P.F. left, the immigrant Muslims would attack them. The Commandant informed the civil administration in Nowgong of the sudden change of heart of the Assamese villagers of the area and their newfound love for the C.R.P.F. He advised strongly that if the C.R.P.F. were withdrawn, there would be a massacre of the Assamese people in that area. Despite his strong assessment of the ground situation, the orders again came to withdraw. By this time it was too late to redeploy the force and the C.R.P.F. continued at their posts. It was at this juncture that the Tiwa and the Assamese people of Jagi road decided to attack the immigrant Muslim villages of Nellie. In a massacre that started on the morning of February 14, a mob of about several hundred Assamese and Tiwas surrounded and attacked all the immigrant Muslim villages of Nellie near Jagi Road. The villagers were taken by surprise and were butchered. Curiously there were hardly any men folk at home. When the mob had satiated their hate, 1658 people had been killed, mostly women, children and old men. In the post mortem of the incident, it was found that a signal had been sent from the Officer in Charge of Nowgong police station that there was intelligence that the Nellie villages might be attacked. It turned out that the Jagi road police station did not take action on this report. The second issue was the absence of young men among the dead. This issue was not probed. The general rumour in the area was that all the young men of Nellie had gone to the Khampur, Jamunamukh areas to attack the Assamese villages there, after the C.R.P.F. withdrew. There are many unanswered questions here. Did the Assamese and Tiwa attackers of Nellie know that the young men of the village had gone south to attack the Assamese villages? Did they also know that the C.R.P.F. were not withdrawing from that area? The officers who operated in the area probably know these answers, but they have not spoken till now.

The Insurgency

This then was the brutal history of the terrible election of February 1983. The last phase of the election was on the 21st. On the 22nd the Prime Minister visited Gohpur and Nellie. It was in the midst of the run up to the election that the A.P.L.A. opened its operations. A C.R.P.F. party was on a routine night patrol in a civil bus. It had crossed Dipota village and had stopped in the middle of a fly-over. There was a burst of fire from the darkness to the left of the over bridge. A Sub Inspector who was leading the patrol was hit by a ricocheting bullet and was killed on the spot. The patrol fired back. Getting the information by wireless, I had gone to the spot at night and reconstructing the situation, we could narrow down the likely ambush spot to a clump of small trees below and to the left of the bridge. After a careful search, a couple of live rounds and some fired cases of cartridges were recovered from the suspected ambush spot. The ammunition was identified as 7.62 rounds fired from an A.K. rifle. This was ominous and was probably the first time that an A.K. rifle was used in Assam. This also meant that the rifle had been obtained from outside the State. That night we searched the houses of some boys who were suspected to be extremists of the Assam movement. In the house of one of these suspects, Arpan Bezbaruah, we found a bunch of empty fired cases and some live cartridges wrapped up in a piece of cloth, concealed inside a banana cluster. Later, we could get ballistic evidence that the empties recovered from the ambush site and from the banana clump were fired from the same gun. Despite our best efforts, we could not recover the A.K. rifle in question. Subsequently, Arpan Bezbaruah was arrested as also his mentor. We could not, however, recover the rifle, nor ascertain its source of supply. The A.P.L.A. surrendered to the Chief Minister in 1985 when the Ahom Gana Parishad formed the Government.

The U.L.F.A. was organised after the horrifying election of 1983. Its mentors were Bhim Kanta Bargohain, an elderly Ahom of Saikhowa Ghat and Badreswar Bargohain of Sonari. Bhim Kanta Bargohain is the real patriarch of the organisation. He has never been interrogated. When I last enquired about his whereabouts, I was told that he was taken by the U.L.F.A. cadres to Bhutan and is their political advisor. The other founder members were Paresh Baruah, the self-styled Commander-in-Chief, Aurobinda Rajkonwar, the Chairman, Pradeep Gogoi, the Vice-Chairman and Golap Baruah, the General Secretary. Aurobinda Rajkonwar was from Lakwa near Sibsagar. Paresh Baruah and Golap Baruah were from Jheraigaon, a village near Dinjon, H.Q.'s of a Mountain Division of the Indian Army. Some Assamese boys had joined the People's Liberation Army of Manipur (P.L.A.) in 1978, been trained in their camps in Myanmar and had fought with them and even died in encounters. There is no record of the Assamese joining with the Naga underground or with the N.S.C.N. Some links were established with the N.S.C.N. at Dimapur in 1983 and the first batch of recruits crossed the international border at Longwa on the Nagaland Arunachal border in late December 1983 and reached the N.S.C.N. camp in Myanmar to a warm welcome from the N.S.C.N. and P.L.A. cadres. Through 1984 the U.L.F.A. built up its cadres and established a network across the Brahmaputra valley. It was only in 1985, when the A.G.P. government was formed that the U.L.F.A. began to operate openly in the Brahmaputra valley. There was a clear nexus between the A.G.P. Government of 1985 and the U.L.F.A. A large-scale extortion network was soon established, with Gauhati University as a base to extort money from the Marwari community. The Gauhati city unit of U.L.F.A. established local H.Q.'s in a department of the University and began summoning all the big Marwari traders of Gauhati. A pall of fear descended on the valley. U.L.F.A., did its homework well, getting details of bank accounts from the banks, financial statements from chartered accountants, and Income Tax officers. None dared to refuse the demands as the police rapidly lost its spine. Demands were then placed giving details of accounts. When someone refused to pay, the result was a quick assassination by a hit group, after which the next victim paid off fast. The link between the A.G.P. and U.L.F.A. was an open fact, as also the link between the A.A.S.U. and the U.L.F.A. Whenever an U.L.F.A. cadre was arrested, the local unit of the A.A.S.U. would call a bandh, while the A.G.P. leaders would intercede with the police and secure his release. U.L.F.A. leaders managed to get police and civil service officers known to be sympathetic to their case posted in crucial positions. The condition of the police became pathetic, and the people at the receiving end, the Marwaris and other businessmen knew that going to the police was meaningless. A few professional police officers continued to perform their duties courageously. They were all marked by the U.L.F.A. The Superintendent of Police of Dibrugarh was one such person. He was under surveillance of the U.L.F.A. for some time, during which period he decided to go to Tinsukhia one day. At the last moment he stayed back, but his wife and children went in his official car ASL 2. The car was tailed by a hit squad of U.L.F.A. that had positioned itself under a large tree near Jheraigaon. When the S.P.'s car went by on the main Dibrugarh-Tinsukhia road, a spotter positioned on the road signalled to the hit car, whose driver immediately swung on to the main road and followed the S.P.'s car. The hit car could not catch up and abandoned the attempt. The assassins, however, positioned themselves again for the return journey. It was late evening when the S.P.'s wife decided to return. It was dark when the car crossed the point where the Jheraigaon road joined the highway. This time the spotter's signal, a flashing torch was quickly acted upon and the hit car swung on to the main road and quickly caught up with the S.P.'s car. As the hit car was overtaking, the killers opened fire with A.K.rifles from the left windows. The two bursts killed the S.P.'s wife, the driver and the gunman. The children of the S.P. were sleeping on his wife's lap and were not hit. As Inspector General of Police

Operations in Assam from November 1990, I had supervised this case and reconstructed the events. The killers did not know that the S.P. had not gone to Tinsukhia. When they fired they thought that the S.P.was in the car.

The Superintendent of Police of Gauhati was a brilliant upright officer. He was high on U.L.F.A.'s hit list. He got information one day that Hirak Jyoti Mohanta, the self-styled vice chief of U.L.F.A. was coming from Jhalukbari to Gauhati. He was able to intercept him and after a tussle, during which a sub inspector was shot, arrest him. After interrogation, he was produced in court under tight security and remanded to judicial custody in Gauhati jail. The C.R.P.F was additionally deployed around the jail to preempt a jailbreak attempt. The U.L.F.A. leadership was extremely upset, as Hirak Jyoti Mahanta was a star for them. Several councils of war were held to decide how to get him out. Ultimately, the U.L.F.A. leaders arrived at a top A.G.P. Minister's house and discussed what was to be done. They were advised that the A.G.P. could not openly intercede and get him released. The Minister then suggested to the U.L.F.A. leaders, that they could kidnap either the General Manager of the North East Frontier Railway, or the General Manager of the Indian Oil Refinery at Noonmati. The U.L.F.A. first attempted to kidnap the General Manager of the N.F.Railway. The Railway Protection Special Force who was guarding him was too alert and they gave up the attempt. They succeeded easily with the General Manager of the Refinery. The Police despite their best efforts could get no clue of his whereabouts. He was ultimately exchanged for Hirak Jyoti Mohanta. In December 1990, after Op Bajrang had begun and U.L.F.A. was on the run, the same Superintendent of Police Gauhati, got information of an U.L.F.A. camp beyond Chandrapur east of Noonmati. He raided the camp and arrested a junior U.L.F.A leader who was in charge of the camp. On interrogation, he broke down and revealed the whole story of the kidnapping of the General Manager of the Refinery. After kidnapping him from his staff car outside the Refinery campus, he was taken to their camp at Chandrapur and then taken east to the Kolong River. From here he was taken in a boat across the Kolong and then further east. He was then taken across the Brahmaputra to North Gauhati by a country boat and kept in the house of a respectable middle class family there. He was shifted to fourteen such houses before finally being released in exchange for the U.L.F.A. leader. The accused recorded his statement before a Magistrate and then the accused and the Magistrate were taken for a local verification reconstructing the whole movement. All the fourteen families admitted that the General Manager was kept with them. Yet during the period of the kidnapping no one had the slightest clue of the location of the kidnapped person. There is a lot of controversy about the U.L.F.A.'s support from the local people. This is just one illustration of the total support that all the people of Assam both urban and rural gave the U.L.F.A. The information of the advice given by a top minister to kidnap one of two General Managers was given to me during interrogation of two top U.L.F.A. leaders independently.

Tea garden managers were an obvious target for extortion for the U.L.F.A. Living in isolation in interior areas, they were easy prey for them. The Managers and Assistant Managers were terrified and the Management paid up as the demands came. Surendra Paul of the Assam Tea

Company was killed ostensibly for dismissing Assamese employees of his garden. The Centre finally had to step in and arrange evacuation of a number of Tea Garden Managers by air from an air base of the Cabinet Secretariat at Doom Dooma. Throughout the period 1985-1990, the U.L.F.A. had a free run of the State. The extortions were from the "outsiders", the Marwaris and other businessmen from outside the state and the Tea Companies. The local Assamese were generally not disturbed. Tea Garden Managers who were Assamese were not, however, exempted. Also, all officers of Oil Companies or Government were asked to "lend" their cars or motorcycles, which were sometimes not returned. No one reported these cases. After Op Bajrang began, hundreds of cars, motorcycles and scooters were recovered and it is only then that the claims were made. During this period the U.L.F.A. floated an organisation called the Jatiya Unnayan Parishad. U.L.F.A. cadres of this group were detailed to educate rural people on the evils of drinking, gambling and other vices. It succeeded in developing a Robin Hood image. It also organised flood control measures by getting the village people to do voluntary labour and build small embankments. All this lasted for some time, but soon the money being collected in crores began to play a role. As the U.L.F.A. began its recruitment drive in 1984-85, two kinds of boys and girls joined. The main group consisted of simple villagers, who went for training and came back toughened and to some extent dedicated. Some of these were highly dedicated and motivated and in encounters later with the Army and Para Military Forces preferred to die rather than be captured. S.S. Lt. Chetia, when cornered by the Forces in a house, shot himself with his Chinese pistol. Then there was Haloi, a Kachin-trained boy, who when cornered in a house, held his grenade to his stomach and pulled the pin and blew himself up. The second group consisted of mainly urban boys who were dropouts from school and were indulging in petty crime. This group was to be the nemesis of U.L.F.A., later.

After the first batches were trained in the N.S.C.N. camps in Myanmar along with cadres of the Nagas and the P.L.A. of Manipur, a liaison was established with the Kachin Independent Organisation (K.I.O.) in the Kachin area of northern Myanmar and hence forward cadres of the N.S.C.N., P.L.A. and the U.L.F.A. were trained with the Kachin Independent Army (K.I.A.). The K.I.A. instructors were battle hardened and tough and they trained the U.L.F.A. cadres well. Boys, who walked up the steep hills of the Kachin country and trained under the K.I.A. instructors, came back lean, muscled and tough. The K.I.O. also deployed the N.S.C.N. and U.L.F.A. cadres with their Brigades to fight the Myanmar army. Many U.L.F.A. cadres died in these fights. Initially the U.L.F.A. could only get 0.30 calibre carbines from Nagaland. When the Kachin connection came through, they were able to buy weapons like G-3 rifles captured from the Myanmar army. They also managed to buy a large number of M-20 Chinese pistols, a limited number of M-21 self-loading rifles and some M-22 rifles, the Chinese version of the A.K. 47. They also got a few M-23, a belt-fed Chinese light machine gun. More than 2000 cadres were trained with the N.S.C.N. in Myanmar and with the K.I.A. Bertil Lintner visited Kachin in 1986-87 and met the S.S. Commander Paresh Baruah at the H.Q.s of the K.I.O.[14] Back in Assam after the training, the cadres spread out and organised themselves into district and tehsil units.

They concentrated on extortion and selected killings of political opponents and of course of those who did not pay, in accordance their demands. In their killings of police and civil officials, their supporters among the government employees actively helped them. Unlike the Naga Underground, they did not have to face a hostile government. Hence they did not have to ambush security force convoys or attack police stations and capture arms. Money was flowing into the U.L.F.A. coffers in unbelievable amounts. There were supporters who converted the rupees extorted to dollars in the Hawala market of Bombay. One such person was Rebati Phukan, a former football referee of Assam. He was from Jheraigaon and related to Paresh Barua and was to play a significant role in the history of the state. Unlike in most insurgencies, where the group organises in the hinterland, strikes in the urban areas and melts away into the forests and remote areas, the U.L.F.A. had a relatively easy genesis. This was to tell on its performance when the Army operations began on November 28, 1990.

Meanwhile, they had set up their General Head Quarters (G.H.Q.) in Lakhipather Reserve Forest located near Digboi. Tactically this was poorly sited. Lakhipather, literally a bountiful paddy field, was located in the midst of paddy fields. Close to the border of Khonsa district of Arunachal Pradesh, there were many sites that were hilly, directly bordering Khonsa district. Such sites would have been tactically better as the rear was inaccessible and also left an escape route. The local police and their superior officers knew that U.L.F.A. had its G.H.Q. at Lakhipather, but no attempt was made to encircle it and capture it. The Assam Police had the ability to do this, as the U.L.F.A. at that time did not have the firepower to defend itself. President's rule was declared on November 28 and army operations commenced the same day. The U.L.F.A.'s link with the A.G.P. Government helped them as the attack on Lakhipather turned out to be a farce. It was obvious that the U.L.F.A. were forewarned, for when the Army went in, only a few second and third line cadres were left to detonate some improvised explosive devices buried in tracks leading to the camp. All the top leaders, with wireless sets and weapons had shifted to a camp at Saraipung on the Khonsa border. For the next three months, the Army did extensive operations all over Assam, mostly cordon and search in villages and towns looking for the first and second line leaders. The U.L.F.A. had never operated in classic guerilla war and went completely on the defensive. They also did not have the firepower. They however had one thing in their favour, complete support from the urban and rural people. This was why virtually no information of the first and second line leaders was available. It was only in chance encounters during cordon and search or on random patrols that a U.L.F.A. boy was apprehended. Where the coordination with the police was good the results were better. A number of second line leaders were soon arrested. In a chance encounter in Dibrugarh, the Army arrested Sourav Gogoi, the District Commander of Dibrugarh. On his leading, more than Rs. one crore was recovered. This was part of the collections from extortions in Dibrugarh and Tinsukhia. It was much later when we interrogated a top leader of U.L.F.A. that we came to know that the collection from Dibrugarh and Tinsukhia amounting to more than Rs. ten crores had not been deposited to the central council. Unfortunately the police did not get a chance to interrogate

Sourabh Gogoi, and he was remanded to judicial custody after his remand in police custody was over. During the period in police custody, he was with the Army. Within days of judicial custody in the district jail of Dibrugarh, Sourabh Gogoi escaped. After this it was decided to set up special jails. Six special jails were notified to keep these high security detenues. All the important U.L.F.A. cadres arrested were kept in these special jails. The jails were all located in cantonment areas and had C.R.P.F. guarding the perimeter. There were no more escapes. It was only by this time that we began to realise that the U.L.F.A. did not have very many arms. A lot of information of the functioning of the organisation had by now been collected and documented. Important cases were transferred to the Special Operations Unit, which had jurisdiction all over the state. By now the extortion net of U.L.F.A. was broken, shops began to function normally. The Congress Party now began to press for the elections to be held, and their main ally was the Principal Advisor to the Government. Those of us who were in the field opposed the holding of elections at this stage when none of the top leaders of the banned U.L.F.A. had been arrested. Our intelligence also said that U.L.F.A. would oppose the elections. It was therefore a big surprise, when suddenly the U.L.F.A., in a press release in April said that they would not oppose the elections. When we discussed this with our contacts in the lower cadres of the U.L.F.A., they were also confused, but informed us that orders to this effect had come from their topmost echelons, but no resaons given. The Army was withdrawn when they were in full cry, breaking their tempo of operations, despite our strenuous objections. OP Bajrang had come to an abrupt end. Within a week the election campaigns started. We thought that the U.L.F.A. would reorganise and start operating again. Strangely, their cadres virtually disappeared from the scene. Our contacts informed us that they had been told to lie low and not operate. Further, they should make themselves scarce from the general scene. They would be told the reason for this later. No further information was forthcoming. Sightings of U.L.F.A. cadres were rare. Chance sightings showed them in remote villages whiling away their time. We were utterly foxed. It was only in December 1991, when we had achieved a breakthrough of sorts with more than 30 second line cadres, either captured or surrendered, that two of the top cadres told us independently during interrogation the story behind the U.L.F.A. agreeing to have the election.

In April 1991, the Army had been conducting an operation in the Saraipung Reserve Forest. Unbeknown to them the S.S. Commander in chief, Paresh Barua was trapped in the cordon. Realising that his escape route to Khonsa area had been cut off, and he might be captured or killed, he hastily sent word for Rebati Phukan, his cousin from Jheraigaon village, who had a link with Hiteswar Saikia, the State Congress leader. Rebati Phukan managed to slip inside the cordon and meet Paresh Barua. He was told to carry a message to Hiteswar Saikia, that the U.L.F.A. would not oppose an election, provided that the Army operations were stopped immediately. Rebati Phukan carried out this mission. With this information, several unexplained incidents earlier fell into place. The sudden stand taken by the Principal Advisor that the Army should be withdrawn and elections should be held was now explainable. This was why the U.L.F.A. virtually disappeared from the scene during the run up to the elections. They surfaced after the elections in a dramatic manner. After the accord in 1985, the Bengali Muslim vote bank had split. This helped the A.G.P. to win. This time after five years of U.L.F.A.'s rule, the Bengali Muslim vote bank reconsolidated and the Congress won. On the date of the swearing in, the U.L.F.A. struck, kidnapping 14 officials, including one I.A.S. officer and a Russian mining engineer. Neither the Central nor the State Intelligence had a clue to this. Our contacts were as foxed as we were. It was one of U.L.F.A.'s high level operation. It was a message to Hiteswar Saikia that the pact was over and the war was on again.

The U.L.F.A. demanded the release of all their important cadres who were in special jails in return for the 14 kidnapped officials. The Chief Minister wanted to accede to the demands. The Director General of Police refused to agree to this and all of us stood by him. We took the stand that releasing arrested cadres would be a sign of weakness and a loss of face for the government. If the kidnapped persons were killed in cold blood, it would go against the U.L.F.A. The Russian mining engineer was killed while he was being kidnapped. It was reported that he snatched a sten gun from one of his kidnappers and he was shot and killed before he could use the weapon. Despite the best efforts of the police, state special branch and central intelligence agencies, not a clue could be obtained of the 13 kidnapped officials. Much later we could ascertain from interrogation of arrested cadres, that all the 13 kidnapped officials were kept in the houses of middle class Assamese people all over the state, and shifted from one house to the other after every three or four days. Not one of these numerous people involved had passed on a clue to the police or intelligence agencies. What better proof could there be of the total support for the U.L.F.A. by the common people of Assam? The Chief Minister wanted to release the U.L.F.A cadres and the Director General of Police continued to oppose this. Finally the Director General of Police went on leave and the U.L.F.A. cadres were released. It was a humiliating blow for the Army and the Police. Without exception the cadres rejoined their comrades, though overtures were made to them by the political leadership to come over ground. The hostages were released one by one. One of them an official from O.N.G.C. was released at the railway gate in Simalguri, but while walking across was shot in the back and killed. This was a dastardly act and cost the U.L.F.A. dear. The Assamese people condemned this senseless killing and the U.L.F.A. lost a measure of support from their own people.

With the withdrawal of the Army, the force levels of Security forces had dropped considerably, and it was difficult to conduct counter-Insurgency operations all over the State. The Army was soon recalled. They redeployed but in depleted strength, in OP Rhino. Gradually, the tempo of counter insurgency operations picked up. In Kamrup district, and particularly in Gauhati, we had considerable success. We were operating as a combined team of two Superintendents of Assam Police and one company of an infantry battalion of the Army. Gradually we began picking up lower level cadres and after careful interrogation, succeeded in turning them around, recruited them in the Police and got them to operate with us. We never allowed them to operate on their own and never gave them any weapons. They operated night and day along with security personnel in civil dress. With their help we succeeded in arresting several second line cadres and one first line cadre. There were some committed cadres who refused to change their stand, but quite a few turned round and joined the group with us. At this point Golap Baruah, the S.S.General Secretary was arrested in Calcutta. His interrogation added a lot of useful information on the U.L.F.A. He and other cadres were all lodged in the special jails. It was at this stage that a virtual bonanza fell into our laps.

One day some of our team of counter guerillas met us and excitedly told us that a group of second line U.L.F.A cadres who had gone to Bangladesh and then to Pakistan had abruptly returned after breaking up with the S.S. Commander Paresh Barua in Bangladesh. They wanted to meet us. Would we be willing? For some time we had been getting whispers that some U.L.F.A. leaders had gone to Bangladesh for help. We could not believe this. Then we got a pamphlet distributed by U.L.F.A. leaders among their cadres, stating that the Assamese people should reconsider their views about immigrant Muslims. They were extremely hard-working farmers and toiled day and night in the fields. The 1983 riots and killings should not be discussed with the immigrant Muslim community. The Assamese should make an effort to understand the culture of the Bengali Muslims who are now Notun Ahomiya.[15] This pamphlet completely foxed us. Later when rumours of the U.L.F.A. going to Bangladesh for help began to circulate, the pamphlet began to make sense. A few days later, a group of five U.L.F.A. boys came to meet us. They told an extraordinary story that their leader with 14 others had been sent to Bangladesh to contact their Army and ask for sanctuary and assistance in their fight against the Indian Government. They were welcomed by officials from their Directorate General of Forces Intelligence (D.G.F.I.) and taken to the Pakistan Embassy in Dacca. Later they were given Bangladeshi names and passports and sent to Karachi in a Bangladesh Biman flight. There they were received by Pakistan I.S.I. officials and taken by air to Peshawar, where they were trained in an Afghan Mujahideen camp. They were trained in weapons and field craft. They were trained to fire the A.K.47, the R.P.D.7.62 L.M.G., and the R.P.G.-7 Rocket launcher. They were also taught how to prepare and set off explosive devices. Back in Bangladesh, they were briefed by a Pakistan I.S.I. officer who directed them to return to Assam and plan and carry out a sabotage of the Noonmati oil refinery. On this they expressed reservations to their S.S. Commander Paresh Barua. They said that sabotaging the oil refinery would be destroying Assam's wealth. There was an argument on this with Paresh Baruah insisting that these orders be carried out. Finally the group of 15 decided to break away from the U.L.F.A. and managed to slip away from the safe house and return to Assam. After a week of debriefing by Intelligence agencies, the group agreed to surrender to the government. It was around this time that one more first line leader, Siddartha Phukan alias Sunil Nath was arrested. He agreed to come over ground after interrogation. At this stage an attempt was made by a Central Intelligence agency to get all the top leaders and some second line leaders to talk to the Prime Minister at Delhi. Golap Baruah was persuaded in jail, and finally the whole group was taken to Delhi. On their return, Golap Baruah was released to contact the S.S. Chairman Aurobinda Rajkunwar and other leaders to come over ground, renounce arms and accept the Indian Constitution. The Council H.Q.s of the U.L.F.A. was now in

Nowgong district. Golap Baruah met the council leaders at Nowgong and Tezpur. On the day he was to report back, he quietly crossed over to Bangladesh, and the other leaders dispersed from the Nowgong area. To us who had handled Golap Baruah, we knew that he was not to be trusted. He had shifty evasive eyes and he would never look at one directly. In typical Assamese rustic humour, a leading U.L.F.A. member told me that the day Golap Baruah was born, 100 jackals died in the forest.

We had been monitoring the developments after Golap Baruah was released and he started meeting the frontline leaders. The S.S. commander was in Bangladesh and he had informed his colleagues, not to agree for talks. We had informed the Government of this decision. We had also told the Director General of Police that Golap Baruah was a slippery customer and could not be trusted. A surrender ceremony was held with the group that had returned from Bangladesh and some others who had been arrested and agreed to come over ground. The government planned to rehabilitate them by organising some cooperatives for them. The group deposited only some of the weapons they had. These were all weapons purchased from the K.I.A, like M-20 pistols, M-21 and G-3 rifles. All were old weapons. The group did not deposit any M-22 rifles. Our information was that the U.L.F.A. had only 15 M-22 rifles, the Chinese version of the A.K.-47. Of these 6 were captured by the Army and Para Military forces during OP Bajrang and OP Rhino.

Meanwhile, the N.S.C.N. (I.M.) had joined the U.L.F.A. and P.L.A in Bangladesh. The I.S.I. of Pakistan with the help of the D.G.F.I. of Bangladesh had set them up in safe houses. More batches of U.L.F.A. had crossed over to Bangladesh and sent to Peshawar for training. Forty-four cadres were trained in Peshawar. Neither the central nor the state intelligence agencies knew of this. Then in early 1992, the Deputy Inspector General of Police Mizoram, informed us that a group of N.S.C.N. (I.M.) was moving south along the eastern border of Mizoram and turning west at Parva, the southern most point of Mizoram, had entered Bangladesh. We could not understand the significance of this movement at that point of time. Then the government got a break. Ten cadres of the N.S.C.N. (I.M.) suddenly came and surrendered to the Border Security Force post at Parva. They were brought to Massimpur and interrogated. They revealed that 250 of them had been sent from Paren in Nagaland to Bandarban in Bangladesh to collect weapons that had been brought to Cox's Bazaar for them. They were to carry them back to Nagaland via Mizoram and Manipur. They had left their camp at Bandarban because of the harsh conditions and long absence from home. It was subsequently revealed that the Pakistan I.S.I. had arranged for weapons to be purchased from the arms bazaar of Thailand, and transportation by coastal steamers to Cox's Bazaar. A few weeks later, the Deputy Inspector General of Police reported that a group of N.S.C.N. (I.M.) were moving along the borders of Mizoram and heading for Manipur. This was presumably the remaining 240 cadres of the N.S.C.N. going back to Nagaland after collecting the weapons dropped at Cox's Bazaar. It was much later that the Government learnt all the facts. Piecing together intelligence and interrogation reports it was discovered that the Pakistan I.S.I. was assisting the N.S.C.N. (I.M.), U.L.F.A., the National Democratic Front of Bodoland (N.D.F.B.) and possibly the P.L.A. to procure arms from the arms bazaar of Thailand. During the period 1992-95, at least three or four consignments of various arms, mainly A.K.47, R.P.D.7.62. L.M.G, R.P.G.-7 Rocket Launchers and 60mm Mortars were brought by this route to Nagaland and thence to Assam for the U.L.F.A. and N.D.F.B. This also explains the escalation in use of weapons against the security forces in Nagaland and Manipur. In Assam too the U.L.F.A. fired an R.P.G.-7 Rocket Launcher at Kalaigaon for the first time. The U.L.F.A. did not suffer from any shortage of weapons after this.

The period 1993-2000 saw erosion in U.L.F.A.'s support base, though its firepower had considerably increased. It also saw very wrong tactics being followed in handling the counter guerrilla groups in fighting the U.L.F.A. The whole issue started with the A.G.P. Government of 1985. A large number of A.A.S.U. volunteers could not be rehabilitated after the accord was signed and the A.G.P. formed the government. The A.G.P. leaders hit upon a bright idea to rehabilitate some of their cadres. More than a thousand coal trucks used to pass through Gauhati every day, coming from Jowai and going to Joghigopa, or directly to Bihar and Delhi. The A.G.P. leaders decided to levy sales tax on each truck. The truckers were to pay the sales tax by depositing a draft along with a challan at the check gate at Jhalukbari. The Sales Tax Commissioner was directed to hand over the challans to a syndicate of former A.A.S.U. volunteers, who would sell them to the truckers. In this way the State would get some revenue and the rehabilitated A.A.S.U.volunteers would be able to earn a living. The whole thing was illegal and immoral. It was also sending a wrong message to the erstwhile A.A.S.U. volunteers. The truckers should not have agreed to this but they had no choice and in any case the profits from transportation of coal was enormous. Each truck was normally overloaded by 3 to 4 tons. Thus was the coal mafia first created in Gauhati. When the Congress took over in June 1991, they took over the Coal Mafia, running it with the same A.A.S.U. cadres. The first group of U.L.F.A. boys who surrendered was rehabilitated in several cooperative societies. After this surrender, the Congress leadership saw to it that all surrenders took place directly before them. Jugal Kishore Mohanta was the U.L.F.A. leader of the Tinsukhia unit. He could not be captured despite our best efforts. We had been told that the collection of Rs. ten crores of the Tinsukhia unit of U.L.F.A.was not handed over to the C.H.Q. by Jugal Kishore Mohanta. He surrendered to the Chief Minister and was allowed to escape scot-free and also keep his weapons with him. Saurabh Gogoi, the killer of Daulat Singh Negi, the gallant Superintendent of Police of Dibrugarh district was arrested by the Army and sent to judicial custody, from where he escaped. He surrendered to the Chief Minister in 1992, and was allowed to go free with his weapons. The security forces despite their best efforts could not arrest Chakra Gohain, the killer of the wife of the earlier Superintendent of Police, Dibrugarh. He also surrendered to the Chief Minister and was allowed to go free without even being interrogated. At one time, right from 1985 to 1992, he was the arms controller of U.L.F.A. All these were now constituted into a general mafia who slowly took over the coal and fish trade of Assam, unnecessarily introducing a middleman into the trade which resulted in the public paying more for the same goods, and prostituting the criminals who had committed murder and were now being used in this nefarious business. The Police were asked to look the other way, while a gang of criminals moved around with their A.K. rifles. Very soon, the mafia diversified their activity by extorting money from the business community, using their weapons to reinforce their demands. This group now began to be called Surrendered U.L.F.A. (S.U.L.F.A.). They were a law unto themselves and acted with impunity, as the Police did not interfere in matters concerning them. They now behaved exactly like the U.L.F.A. did from 1985 to 1990; only this time they had direct political patronage. The S.U.L.F.A were also used to locate the U.L.F.A. cadres. In this they were not very successful, except when they were given specific tasks of assassinating some of them. The worst-case scenario was when they were tasked to kill the innocent relatives of some hard-core U.L.F.A. cadres. In two cases the mother and sister of U.L.F.A. cadres were killed in cold blood. No dirtier form of fighting can be imagined. And in this case it was the Government not terrorists who were responsible. What a far cry from what Sir Frank Kitson had written on Counter Guerrilla Warfare.[16] In 1996, when the A.G.P. returned to power, the Mafia quickly changed sides and was now taken over by the A.G.P. leadership. It was during this period that the S.U.L.F.A. gained the notoriety decribed above. The endnote to this thoroughly unsavoury story is what happened when the Congress returned to power in 2001. The coal and fish mafia again changed hands but was run by a leader of the Congress Party from Delhi!

In 1988, probably seeing the U.L.F.A. develop, a mainly Christian group of Boros from Udalguri founded the Boro Security Force (Bd.S.F.) Initially based in Udalguri, the force soon spread to Kokrajhar. Unlike the All Boro Students Union, the Boro Peoples Action Committee, and the armed wing of this group, the A.B.S.U. Volunteer Force, The Bd.S.F. wanted total independence from India. They crossed into Bhutan at two points in Udalguri area and set up camps there. In 1991 the U.L.F.A. leadership finding that Bd. S.F. had established camps in Bhutan, asked for a meeting with them. This was agreed to and two top leaders of U.L.F.A. attended a meeting with the Bd.S.F. in their camp across the border in Bhutan near Badlapara tea garden. At this meeting the Bd.S.F. agreed to U.L.F.A. setting up camps in Bhutan. From that time there were good relations between U.L.F.A. and Bd.S.F, despite the fact that the A.B.S.U. and the B.P.A.C. were enemies of U.L.F.A. The relation of these two insurgent groups with the Bhutan Government was symbiotic. In 1990, the Bhutan Government after assessing the threat of Nepalese immigration into Bhutan, had decided to make 1958 the cut off year for giving citizenship to its Nepalese settlers. After passing the necessary laws, the Bhutan Government started evicting the Nepalese. The evicted Nepalese tried to enlist the support of their pre-1958 brethren to fight a hit and run war with the Bhutan Government. It was soon after this that the Bd.S.F. approached the Bhutan Government for permission to set up their camps in Bhutan. The Assamese and the Boros had no love for the Nepalese. Already a large number of Nepalese had settled in Assam. When the Bd.S.F.and later the U.L.F.A. asked the Bhutan Government for permission to set up camps in the remote jungles close to the Indian border, they gladly permitted it. The U.L.F.A. and the Bd.S.F. became the unofficial border guards of the Bhutan Government against Nepalese reinfiltration. This was confirmed to me by several top-level sources from Bhutan. After the first agreement between the U.L.F.A. the two groups did not have any major disagreements. In fact the relationship became stronger, with the U.L.F.A. taking the Bd.S.F. to Bangladesh. Later Ranjan Daimary, the founder member of the group, shifted to a safe house in Dacca. The Bd.S.F also became a beneficiary of the arms being brought from Thailand. The Bd.S.F. later changed its name to the the National Democratic Front of Boroland (N.D.F.B.) The U.L.F.A. soon set up several camps in Bhutan opposite Kamrup, Nalbari, Barpeta and Kokrajhar districts.

The U.L.F.A. and probably the N.D.F.B. invested a lot of their funds collected from extortion in Bhutan. The businessmen of Bhutan benefited from this and naturally lobbied for them with their Government. In 1992, a top-level source of mine told me that if we wanted to operate inside Bhutan, we should take permission from their government through our External Affairs Ministry. We did get permission once, but when we conducted an operation inside Bhutan, we found the camps empty. When I got back to my source, he told me that after their government had given the permission, the insurgent group was informed. The message was clear, that the Bhutan Government had an indirect link with the two insurgent groups. As the years passed both the insurgent groups increased their camps. The U.L.F.A.'s Central H.Q.s was established at Deothang and the General H.Q.s at Sakuni in Samdrup Jhankar district. Four training camps were also set up. They also established camps near the tri junction of Assam, West Bengal and Bhutan at Khalikhola in Geylephug district. It was here that cadres of the Kamtapur Liberation Organisation were trained when U.L.F.A. established a link with them. The strength of U.L.F.A. cadres in Bhutan at any one time was nearly 1000. By this time the link with the Bhutan Government was fully established. The U.L.F.A. were using the diplomatic bags of the Bhutan Government for sending money to their contacts abroad. The U.L.F.A. managed to go to Tibet and possibly China from Bhutan. This we know from interrogation reports. This they could not have done without government help. In fact an official from the Bhutan Government accompanied the U.L.F.A. leader to Tibet to meet Chinese officials for purchase of arms. In 1995 a consignment of arms, A.K. 47, A.K. 56 and R.P.D 7.62 L.M.G. and ammunition arranged from China was delivered from a Chinese naval ship off the coast of Cox's Bazaar and transshipped into a hired vessel. The second consignment of arms was to be delivered on the Tibet border at Tremo La in the Chumbi valley. A senior U.L.F.A. cadre went to this remote outpost to take delivery of the consignment accompanied by a senior official from the Bhutan Foreign Ministry. At the last moment the Bhutan Government asked their officer not to accept the consignment as the Indian Embassy in Bhutan got wind of the deal. The party had to return. Later Paresh Baruah himself went to the Tibet border and brought the consignment of 170 A.K.56 rifles and 235 pistols to the Deothang camp. This was in April 1999. The Communication net of U.L.F.A. is controlled from their Mobile Station H.Q.s located near Pema Gyatchal town. Another relay centre was the Joimati Communication Centre near Bhangtar. The sets were all Japanese. By the end of 2000, U.L.F.A. had a cadre strength of 1,400 active personnel, organised in 3 battalions, with plans to have two more. They had 600 A.K. series rifles, 400 R.P.D.7.62 L.M.G.s, 400 pistols, 13 R.P.G.-7 Rocket Launchers and three 60mm Mortars. They had, however, lost the goodwill of the people of Assam. The main reason was the large-scale corruption that had permeated the organisation. Several cadres had surrendered to the political leadership and obtained their protection after misappropriating extorted money and then under the patronage of the politicians continued to extort money and live in a lavish style. This naturally had a very negative effect on the people of Assam. They began to lose faith in the organisation. In the formative years, extortion was from the Marwaris and other outside businessmen. By the late 1990s, the Assamese people were also included in the extortion net. The large majority of the rural and urban Assamese had felt that the U.L.F.A. was their last hope. In 1999, as the Kargil war progressed, the U.L.F.A. made a call to support Pakistan in the war. This was a categorical mistake. It was just at this time that the body of Capt. Jiten Gogoi, who had died gallantly on the heights of Kargil, was brought home to an emotional funeral. U.L.F.A.'s call went down very negatively with the Assamese people. One of the reasons that the organisation continues to survive is because of the economic conditions of the people. A large number of young boys and girls drop out of school, because of the extremely poor quality of education. Quite a number drop out from college too. This huge pool of unemployed youth is a continuing market for U.L.F.A. This is one reason why recruitment to U.L.F.A. has not flagged.

Remedies

What is the answer for Assam? The Assamese have always maintained that the Centre has neglected them. This is true. The greatest betrayal, however, was by their own A.G.P. In 1985, they had begun with a clean slate, and they had the whole world at their feet. Throughout the Foreigners' agitation, the party in power at Delhi had tried their best to purchase them. They had withstood all blandishments. When they came to power, they withstood temptation for three months. Then they royally succumbed and sold themselves to the business community, lock, stock and barrel. In their first term some of their Ministers did perform. Roads were considerably improved. It was in their second term that they threw all caution to the winds. I had toured extensively in all the border areas of Nalbari, Barpeta, Bongaigaon, Kokrajhar and Dhubri districts from 1998 to 2000 and interacted with the District officials. In all these districts the politicians from Gauhati diverted 95 per cent of development money, during this period. In one village where tubewells had been dug on paper, the villagers told me that it was the birthright of politicians to take a major share of all such funds. It was an immigrant Muslim village and the Diwani system of the community renders the people as total serfs. For them their Diwani is akin to God. The Diwani is usually an influential landlord who intercedes and bribes the revenue officials of the District on revenue, land, forests, crime and related matters. His word is law in his area. Driving from Dhubri through Kokrajhar, Bongaigaon, Barpeta and Nalbari during the off-season one found the fields fallow throughout. It was only in the area north of Rangiya that one could see green fields. Here the waters of the Bor Nadi channelled through canals from a barrage irrigated the whole area up to Goreswar. The Assamese and Boros could take two crops in a year. A barrage constructed near Baghmara in Barpeta district was not commissioned because the canals had not been made. Probably the situation has not changed till today. In 1983, the Dhansiri river flowing between Bhutan and Arunachal Pradesh was being dammed at a place called Bhairabkhund just beyond the point where it flowed out from Bhutan into India. Later in 1991, I saw the same project abandoned after the dam was constructed. The canals had not yet been constructed. This project was in the same condition in 2000. The Brahmaputra valley has a large number of streams and rivers flowing in from the Himalayas in the north and from the Garo, Khasi, Jaintia, Mikir, North Cachar and the Naga hills from the south. While the rivers cannot be easily dammed, it is feasible to construct barrages or weirs across the smaller streams, and construct canals, which can irrigate the area downstream. The Dhansiri project was one such scheme. So was the barrage constructed near Baghmara in Barpeta District. The only scheme that was successfully constructed was the barrage across the Bor Nadi north of Goreswar. All the villages south of this barrage were irrigated by the water stored by this barrage and every farmer of this area was able to cultivate two crops of paddy, besides growing mustard or vegetables as a third crop. From Kokrajhar to Dhemaji and Silapather, a distance of more than 700 kilometres, the only canal irrigation system is that of the Bor Nadi. Except for the farmers who lived downstream from this barrage, no one in this whole stretch of 700 odd kilometres can cultivate two crops. In the south bank, there is not a single similar irrigation scheme. This is why Assam, despite its surplus water resources has had no green revolution after more than 55 years of independence. I still remember when I first saw the Dhansiri project at Bhairabkhund, the local farmers told me that in Assam dams are constructed for the benefit of the engineers not the farmers.

Agriculture is the mainstay of Assam's economy. While the all India average for the area under agricultural use is 64 per cent, the equivalent area in Assam is only 44 per cent.

Only 7 per cent of arable land has irrigation facilities. 80 per cent of irrigation projects are in the doldrums. In 1995-96 out of 81 crores allotted to the irrigation department 71 crores was spent on salaries. The balance presumably was spent on office expenses, contingencies, etc. Rice is the principal food crop, its cultivation occupying three-fourths of the total cropped area. The average productivity of rice in 1995-96 was 1,350 kgs. per hectare, which is lower than the national average. Fertiliser consumption in Assam is less than one-fifth of the national average. While the consumption of electricity in the agricultural sector was about 30 per cent of the total consumption, in Assam it was only 3 per cent. Manipur and Tripura have done far better in agricultural production. The result is that despite having very fertile land, Assam has to import food products worth 1,500 crores every year. The ultimate humiliation is that even fish is imported from Andhra Pradesh. Low agricultural production is blamed on recurring floods. The fact is that floods normally do not affect more than 30 per cent of cultivable land. Only 10 per cent of the land is under forests. If the remaining 60 per cent is utilised properly the state can become self-sufficient in food production.[17]

The youth of Assam have learnt that with the present education system, 70 per cent of students will drop out by the 10th class itself. There are no jobs for them, neither in the government nor in the private sector. They have seen the U.L.F.A.'s extortion net. A sizeable percentage of these dropouts join U.L.F.A. not out of any ideology, or patriotic feelings, which have long since been abandoned, but out of necessity. U.L.F.A. pays them a small salary, and after training you may get a gun. Then you can extort money, some of which you can keep for yourself. You also have a lot of power. In the event of being killed, U.L.F.A. pays some money to the parents.

The Central Government has a formidable task to set things right in Assam. The State Government cannot do this by themselves. The Centre must understand that to bring back a measure of normalcy they have to accept several self-evident truths. The first is that corruption in the State Government cannot be eradicated whichever political party rules. The second is that no counter-insurgency is going to work unless the people get a measure of good clean government. The third is that a long-term plan should be devised and implemented for improving and making the educational system practical and better. The fourth is that 100 per cent funds of rural development should reach the ground. For this, there should be a mechanism of checking that funds have been translated to schemes on the ground.

The Central Government has a very good instrument to see that development and administration moves along the right lines in the Northeast. This is the Northeastern Council. (N.E.C.) It is known to every one that all the Chief Ministers of the Northeastern States oppose the allotment of funds to the N.E.C. tooth and nail. The reason is simple. Funds allotted to the N.E.C. means, that much less funds for swiping. The N.E.C. since its inception did well, except for a spell, when the politicians lobby managed to get a corrupt and servile head for it. This was corrected when the last incumbent, an upright officer was posted despite the politicians' lobby desperately campaigning against his posting. The whole scheme being suggested will be neutralised if the wrong man is posted to the N.E.C. The

Centre must ensure that an honest upright officer of proven integrity is posted as the Secretary of the N.E.C. His subordinate officers must also be chosen as carefully. Now, to the actual mechanism of the plan. Before establishing a counter-insurgency grid, the Public Distribution System should be cleaned up. It must be ensured that rice, wheat, sugar and kerosene oil is available in sufficient quantity at the correct price in every village and every locality of all towns in the state. This can never be ensured by the State, because the personnel of the Food and Civil Supplies Department are so corrupt that it will be impossible to get them to perform honestly. In any case, the Centre sends all civil supplies to the State. Why should the Centre then not distribute them to the people directly? This task should be given to the N.E.C. It should be ensured in the process that the Supply officials of the States do not come on deputation to the N.E.C. No counter-insurgency operation will be productive unless this is ensured. If the people know that their government is clean, they will cooperate and even put up with the harsh operational necessities. But if they see that the government is corrupt, they will not cooperate with the Security Forces because they will feel that the operations are only to perpetuate a corrupt regime. If it is not possible to give the P.D.S. to the N.E.C., then President's rule should be invoked to clean up the P.D.S. It must be understood that in all the Northeastern States, 70 per cent of all rice brought by the F.C.I. is diverted to the black market. Wheat is diverted wholesale from the railheads, but full transportation is claimed for lifting it to the state capitals of Nagaland, Manipur, Mizoram, and Arunachal Pradesh. In Assam, it is diverted wholesale to the rice mills. Consumption of wheat is virtually nil in the Northeast as all are rice eaters.

The second emphasis should be on Rural Development. Except for Tripura, which is one of the cleanest states of India, 70 to 95 per cent of rural development funds sent directly to the Deputy Commissioners of the Northeastern States are swiped by devious means by an unholy nexus of politicians, bureaucrats, and insurgents. This task should also be entrusted to the N.E.C. A mechanism should be developed to see that the Accountant General monitors the expenditure and ensures that the money allotted is translated on the ground in physical terms. To ascertain that these two items are properly carried out, sufficient security forces should be placed at the disposal of the N.E.C. Once the P.D.S. and the Rural Development work is on a level plane, counter-insurgency operations can commence. Their first action in Assam is to defang the S.U.L.F.A. All the surrendered U.L.F.A. boys and girls should be detained and their weapons seized. Subsequently their cases should be examined and all of them responsible for heinous crimes prosecuted. The coal and fish mafia must be disbanded and political patronage withdrawn. This can be done only by enforcing President's rule. Once the burden of S.U.L.F.A. and the coal and fish mafia is lifted from the population, their cooperation with the Security Forces will improve. The main U.L.F.A. can now be tackled. The main objective should be to seize their weapons. More than 80 per cent of their weapons are in Bhutan. The Assamese intelligentsia wants that the Centre should talk to the U.L.F.A. There should be no question of talking to a bunch of brigands, who have long since thrown their ideology to the winds and whose leaders have invested the funds collected by extortion in personal enterprises. The next step should be to transfer all irrigation schemes both major and minor to the N.E.C. and take them up on a war footing. Assam has lost out more than 30 years because of the venality of their politicians and bureaucracy. The victims have been their own people. It is only after small dams and weirs are constructed below the foothills to the north and the south that the farmers who live downstream can think of two paddy crops in a year. Assam can then have her long awaited green revolution.

The last step in this Counter-Insurgency Module is to revamp the education system in Assam. This is a major step and needs considerable planning and funds. The plan envisaged will yield results only after ten years. Under the guidance of the N.E.C. several trusts in India should be asked to set up schools in every small town of the State. The funding should be from the Central Government, but each trust should be allowed to implement its own educational pattern as in their schools in Delhi or elsewhere. The different trusts should be asked to set up their schools and N.E.C. should only channel the funds to them. This should bring about a revolution in education in the State. The funds invested by the Centre would have been profitably invested, far better than pouring funds to the State which are swiped by the notorious coterie of the politician, the bureaucrat and the businessman, hoping in the end that the people will get corrupted and too soft to fight any further.

References

1. Edward Gait. *The History of Assam*. Chapter-2. Page-22.
2. Ibid.
3. S.K. Bhuyan. *Anglo-Assamese Relations,1711-1826*. Chapters 8, 9 and 10.
4. Ibid.

5. John Butler. *Travels and Adventures in the Province of Assam.*

6. Amalendu Guha. *Planter Raj to Swaraj*. Chapter 2. Page 39.

7. Tilottama Misra. *Literature and Society in Assam*. Page 195.

8. Girin Phukan. *Assam's Attitude to Federalism*. New Delhi, 1984.

9. Jnanath Bora. *Kamrup aru Bharatvarsha.* Awahon (Assamese) Vol.8, No.3, Calcutta 1936.

10. Census of India. 1961.

11. Udayan Misra. *The Periphery Strikes Back*. Chapter 5. Page 123. Indian Institute of Advanced Study. Simla.

12. Tilottama Misra. "Assam: A Colonial Heartland." *Economic and Political Weekly*. Bombay. Vol.-15. No 39.

13. Udayan Misra. Ibid. Chapter-5. Page, 132.

14. *The Land of Jade*. Bertil Lintner.

15. Sanjukta Mukti Bahini, Ahom. Prachar Patra 1992.

16. Frank Kitson. *Bunch of Five*.

17. Dr. Gulshan Sachdeva. *Assam's Economy,Past Present and Future.*

The Damned of the Earth

The Chakmas today live along the eastern borders of Tripura, along the western border of Mizoram and in Arunachal Pradesh. Their total population in these three states will not total more than two lakhs. In Tripura they are not discriminated against, but they live in the most difficult area of that state, along a strip of land bordering the Chittagong Hill Tracts [C.H.T.]. In the north, in Dholai district, this stretch has no roads and the Chakmas who inhabit this area have to walk two days to reach the nearest road head to get supplies of rice and kerosene. They have no access to medical care or education. The only other inhabitants of this area are the Border Security Force, who have border outposts [B.O.P.] along this inhospitable stretch. Helicopters maintain these B.O.P.s. The most dangerous threat is from cerebral malaria. Each B.S.F. post keeps Plasmodium Falsifarum identification kits. Anyone developing a fever is immediately tested for the parasite and if found positive is immediately evacuated. Despite all the precautions taken, the B.S.F. still take casualties. Further south, in Udaipur district, the border road from Katalcherra to Boalkhali and S.K. Para lends some measure of civilised support to the Chakmas who live along this stretch. Though living at the edge of civilisation, they are at least not discriminated against by the government. This is not the case in the two other states where the Chakmas live.

In Mizoram, the Chakmas probably gradually drifted and settled along the borders of the erstwhile Mizo Hills

district of Assam, from their original home in the C.
Today they are about ninety thousand to one lakh scatt
along the western border of Mizoram State from Tuipu
in the north to Parva in the south. In Mizoram today
are second-class citizens. They are discriminated agains
all grounds. Fortunately they were given a District Cou
by the Central Government, when Mizoram was still a U
Territory. This is still resented by the Mizo political lea
The District Council however covers only one-third of
Chakma population in the state, and the Mizo lea
steadfastly refuse to consider extending the District Co
to the whole of the Chakma population. In the areas out
the District Council, as the older teachers retire, new teac
are not appointed, there is no college, and health
facilities do not exist. The Chakma population sile
suffers. The Mizo leaders have forgotten the way As
neglected their district for 20 years, and are treating
Chakmas worse than the Assamese treated them.

There are about one lakh Chakmas in Aruna
Pradesh, where they were settled way back in the 19
when they were displaced by the construction of a
across the Karnaphuli river at Kaptai in the C.H.T. H
again the Arunachal political leaders treat them as sec
class citizens. They have been denied citizenship, tho
the Government of India settled them there as refugees n
than thirty years ago. Bangladeshi migrants, who migr
illegally into India from 1950 to March 1971, have b
granted citizenship, while the Chakmas who were acce
as refugees and settled in India by the government have
got citizenship.

The C.H.T. is an area of 13,295 square kilometres ir

southeastern part of Bangladesh. It is bordered on the east by the Arakan and Chin states of Myanmar and Mizoram state of India, and on the west by Tripura. From time immemorial, the C.H.T. have been inhabited by 13 indigenous ethnic groups collectively identified as the Jumma people. They are the Chakma, Marma, Pankhua, Reang, Tripura, Tanchangya, Mro, Murung, Lushai, Khumi, Chak, Khayang, and Bawm. They are distinct and different from the Bengali Hindu and Muslim population of East Bengal in respect of race, language, culture, religion and ethnicity. The British annexed the C.H.T. in 1860, and created an autonomous district, the Chittagong Hill Tracts, within undivided British Bengal. In 1900, the British enacted an act to protect the Jumma people from economic exploitation by non-indigenous people and to preserve their traditional cultural and political institutions based on customary laws and common ownership of land. Throughout the British period the 1900 Act functioned as a safeguard for the Jumma people prohibiting migration of the non-indigenous people to the C.H.T. In 1947 Radcliffe ceded the C.H.T. district to Pakistan, when the Indian subcontinent was partitioned on the basis of religion into Islamic Pakistan and secular India, though the district was 98.5 per cent Buddhist and Christian, and against the express wishes of the Jumma people. On August 15, 1947 Chakma youths under the leadership of Sneha Kumar Chakma hoisted the Indian tricolour at Rangamati, while in the south, the Marmas hoisted the Burmese flag at Bandarban. Six days later the Pakistanis lowered the Indian tricolour at gunpoint.

From the beginning the Pakistanis discriminated against the Jumma people, in jobs, business and education.

The Government of Pakistan amended the 1900 Act several times, against the wishes of the Jumma people. The government then constructed a dam on the Karnaphuli river at Kaptai, inundating 1036 square kilometres of land and displacing about one lakh Chakmas. It was these Chakmas who were resettled in Arunachal Pradesh. Then came the liberation struggle of the Bangladeshis against Pakistan in 1971. The Jumma people did not participate in this liberation struggle; neither did they side with the Pakistanis, as did the Jamaat-e-Islami of Bangladesh. As soon as the Pakistanis withdrew, the Mukti Bahini went on the rampage against the Jummas in the C.H.T. On February 15, 1972, a delegation of the Jumma people led by M.N. Larma called on Sheikh Mujibur Rehman and asked for autonomy for the C.H.T., retention of the C.H.T. regulation of 1900, recognition of the three rajas of the Jumma people, and a ban on the influx of non-Jummas into the C.H.T. All these demands were rejected, and in March 1972, M.N. Larma formed the Jana Samhiti Samiti [J.S.S.]

In the late 1970s, President Zia started settling Bangladeshis from the plains in the C.H.T. In the beginning the government did not make this public. It was only much later that the government acknowledged this. The settlement was very cleverly implemented, by settling the plains people in-between the tribal villages. By 1981 Bangladeshis from the plains equal to more than one-third the population of tribals, had been resettled in the C.H.T. When peaceful overtures to the government failed, the J.S.S. took to arms, and started an armed wing, the Shanti Bahini, on January 7, 1973. The first attack of the Shanti Bahini was on a police post at Bilaichari on May 5, 1976. Initially the Shanti Bahini started their actions with weapons left behind by the Pakistani army. Later they were able to procure weapons from across the border where they set up camps. It is reported that the Shanti Bahini had got some training from the Myanmarese army and some Shanti Bahini cadres disguised as Myanmarese soldiers were also trained by the Chinese. Meanwhile in the C.H.T., a series of skirmishes took place between the Bangladesh army and the Shanti Bahini. The Bangladesh army was first inducted in C.H.T. in October 1976. The civilian population in the C.H.T. suffered the insurgency for more than 20 years. While the army committed several atrocities against the Jumma people, the Bangladeshi settlers suffered at the hands of the Shanti Bahini. While conducting counter-insurgency operations, the Jumma people were often detained and tortured. There were extra judicial executions, tortures and rapes. It is reported that the Shanti Bahini killed 343 army and police personnel. The army killed 268 insurgents, while 238 Jumma people were killed. The Shanti Bahini killed 1054 Bangladeshi settlers, despite the protection given to them by the government. From these figures it can be seen that the Shanti Bahini were holding their ground and even had an advantage over the army.

During this period there was a government-sponsored attempt at converting the Jumma people to Islam. This was organised by Al-Rabita, a Saudi Government-funded N.G.O. The Jamaat-e-Islami, a religious and fundamentalist group) worked in close liaison with the army. Besides trying to convert the Jumma people to Islam, there have also been several incidents of destruction of religious institutions. By 1986 more than 50 Buddhist temples were burnt. Since 1980 there have been 13 instances of massacres of the Jumma people by Bangladeshi settlers with the security forces looking on. Frustrated at the attacks of the Shanti Bahini, the Bangladeshi settlers began to take it out on the Jumma people. The figure of Jumma people killed by the Bangladeshi settlers and the security forces has been grossly reduced. Actually in each of the 13 massacres listed, more than 60 to 70 innocent Jumma people were killed. In many cases the dead bodies were not even recovered. Ultimately a large number of Jumma people, unable to bear the atrocities fled to Tripura. They migrated in waves. They were unfortunately not given refugee status by the United Nations. This was indeed very unfortunate. The Rohingyas, who were driven out by Myanmar, and the supporters of Aung San Su Kyi's League for Democracy driven out by Myanmar were both granted refugee status by the U.N.H.C.R. The hapless Chakmas who had fled from their homeland were housed in slums of bamboo shacks, without sanitation and minimum standards of cleanliness. I had seen these camps and was ashamed that human beings were being kept in such primitive conditions. Their allowance was a pittance, barely enough to keep body and soul together.

In 1997 after Sheikh Hasina and her Awami League came to power, after protracted negotiations a peace treaty was signed between the Jana Samhati Samiti, which was a total sell out of the Jumma people. The Bangladesh Government did not accept the main issue of returning the Bangladeshi settlers from the C.H.T. All that was conceded was that the C.H.T. would have a tribal head who would have the status of a Cabinet Minister. His deputy would however be a settler from the plains. Naturally a faction of the J.S.S refused to accept this agreement, and remained behind in India. The 50,000 odd refugees who had been treated so shabbily trekked back to the C.H.T. only to find that the Bangladeshi settlers were even more firmly entrenched than before. Despite several meetings in 1997, the year the Jumma refugees trekked back, and in 1998, 1999 and 2000 the agreement could not be finalised. The government has till date, not transferred to the Regional Council, powers provided under the accord. As a result, the government is still directly administering the C.H.T. The Land Commission which was to oversee the resettling of the refugees on their respective homesteads and land has not yet been set up. Only 29 of the 500 military camps have been withdrawn from the C.H.T. Bangladeshi Muslims from the plains continue to be settled in the C.H.T.

When Sheikh Hasina started the peace talks with the J.S.S., Khaleda Zia's opposition party of opposed the talks and the agreement later arrived at. In 2001, Khaleda Zia's party, the B.N.P. won the elections in a coalition with the Jamaat-e-Islami. The Jumma people were naturally supporters of Sheikh Hasina's party, the Awami League. The minority Hindus were also supporters of Sheikh Hasina. With the victory of the B.N.P., a wave of violence was unleashed against the Hindus as well as the Jumma people, for having supported the Awami League. The latest in a series of such incidents is the attack on Madarbania village near Ukhia. This is a small village of Chakmas wedged between the hills and the sea. A temple, which had been constructed by the Chakmas, was destroyed in a cyclone in 1994. When they tried to rebuild it after some years, the

Bangladeshi Muslims objected. The local Awami League M.P. intervened and negotiated an agreement. As soon as the B.N.P. Party came to power, the local Bangladeshi Muslims attacked the Chakmas of the village when they were laying a foundation stone for their Buddhist temple. This led to a riot in which one Muslim was killed. In the retaliation that followed, the local government looked aside as the mob attacked the village. All the males of the village fled to the forest. A Chakma woman, Chanio Chakma has come forward and testified in the district court at Cox's Bazaar. Several Chakma women were raped. Chanio Chakma courageously beat off her attackers and has filed a complaint against 11 named attackers all of whom are supporters of Khaleda Zia's B.N.P.

The biggest mistake made by the Chakmas was in agreeing to negotiate with Sheikh Hasina's Government. It was crystal clear to those who were deployed on the border with Bangladesh that Sheikh Hasina's writ did not run very much beyond her own secretariat. The Bangladesh army and police and civil bureaucracy were against the minority Hindus and Buddhists. We in the B.S.F. had specific evidence of camps of the U.L.F.A., N.S.C.N. [I.M.], N.L.F.T., A.T.T.F. and other insurgent groups in the C.H.T. Interrogation reports of arrested insurgents gave us specific locations of camps. We even had photographs of these camps seized from arrested insurgents. When such information was given to our counterparts, all that the nearest Bangladesh Rifles unit would do was to go to the camp and tell the insurgent group to shift their camp. At the next border meeting we would be told that no such camps existed at the places mentioned.

It is quite clear now that there is no hope for the Chakma people. They are doomed to extinction. They were doomed from the time that Jawaharlal Nehru agreed to let Pakistan have the C.H.T., after promising Sneha Kumar Chakma, the representative of the Parbattya Chattogram Jana Samity, that the Bengal Boundary Commission had no jurisdiction over the C.H.T. Sneha Kumar Chakma had met Sardar Patel, and Jawaharlal Nehru in July 1947 and was promised by both, that C.H.T. would remain with India. Then on July 8, 1947, when the Indian Independence Act was published, it showed that Radcliffe had not listened to the submissions of the two Hindu members of the Bengal Boundary Commission, Justice Bijon Mukherjee and Charu Biswas, that C.H.T. should be with India. Sneha Kumar ran to Delhi after hoisting the Indian Tricolour at Rangamati on August 15, 1947, to meet the Indian leaders to try and revise Radcliffs decision. He met Sardar Patel, who told him that he was with him but he should meet Jawaharlal Nehru. It took 50 days for Sneha Kumar Chakma to meet Nehru. When he finally got an audience and told Nehru the C.H.T. should be with India, and the Chakmas were ready to fight for this and would India help with arms, Nehru rose in anger and shouted, "Do you propose to bring India under foreign rule again?" That decision sounded the death knell for the hapless Chakmas.

Porous Borders, Perfidious Neighbours - Security Threat from Bangladesh

Introduction

Bangladesh was born with considerable euphoria. This was mainly among the politicians who were in power then and the bureaucrats who executed the policy objectives. This euphoria has continued and echoes along the corridors of power even today despite the continuously perfidious behaviour of the Bangladesh Government. This totally misplaced sympathy is particularly seen among a group of officials who have handled Bangladesh, and among some public figures who are academics and who are unaware of the ground realities. It is not that the government does not have any inputs from the Intelligence Bureau or the Border Security Force. The Home Ministry is full of reports of the way the Bangladesh Government has been subverting the country. As late as 2001, I remember attending a reception for officials of a Defence Institute of Bangladesh and senior officials talking nostalgically of the role of the Indian Army in liberating Bangladesh. Those who have been visiting Bangladesh and dispassionately watching the developments there ever since Sheikh Mujibur Rehman was killed and Gen. Ziaur Rehman took over as President have a very different tale to tell. The Liberation War was in 1971, a long way off, and the people of Bangladesh have forgotten the role played by the Indian Army. Sadly, they have even forgotten their own heroes and the lakhs of people who were brutally killed by the Pakistan Army and the Razakhars, they have forgotten the thousands of women and girls who were raped and killed, they have forgotten the moving words of Rabindranath Tagore inscribed on the dignified memorial to the lakhs of martyrs of the Liberation War at Sawar-

"So much blood of the brave,
Tears of mothers,
Will the price of all this be lost in the dust of the Earth?"

Sadly, the rulers of Bangladesh and except for a handful of intellectuals, even the people of Bangladesh have forgotten the price of all the costly sacrifices in the dust of the Earth. The evidence of all this is there for any one to see. The Jamaat-e-Islami who sided with Pakistan during the genocide of the Liberation War today has seventeen seats in the Parliament with two Ministers. The Hindu and Buddhist population that was over seventy lakhs in 1971 is now probably less than ten lakhs, and diminishing daily. This is a probable figure as the Bangladesh Government refuses to publish the figures of the minority population. The Chakmas who were about seven lakhs living in the Chittagong hill tracts are today a minority in their homeland, because an equal number of plains Muslims were transplanted and settled interspersed among the tribal villages. This policy was initiated by Sheikh Mujibur Rehman and carried out by Gen. Ziaur Rehman. The Chakmas are a dying race, clearly on the road to extinction. The plight of the other smaller tribes, like the Mogs, the Rakhines and the Buams is even worse.

The security threat from Bangladesh is threefold. The first and the most serious is demographic. The government as a policy encourages and abets migration into India. It is the only nation that pushes its citizens at gunpoint across the border. The second is the continuous threat of destabilisation it holds out to India in abetting and aiding more than a dozen insurgent groups of the Northeast. The third is the support it gives to Islamic fundamentalist groups in infiltrating them into India with arms and explosives for subversion. It is today a base for the Al Qaida, the Jamiat-e-Ulema-e-Islam (J.U.M.), the Harkat-ul-Mujahideen (H.U.M.) and the Harkat-ul-Jihad-e-Islami (H.U.J.I.)

Policing the Borders

The international border (I.B.) in the East, with East Pakistan, and in the West, with West Pakistan, was guarded since partition by armed police battalions of the respective State Police Forces. This was a very unsatisfactory state of affairs, as the States had neither the expertise nor the finances to ensure proper guarding of the I.B. countries with soft democratic governments cannot guard international borders strictly. The Mexican border with the United States is porous. So are the borders of so many western democracies. It is only the totalitarian countries that have successfully guarded their international borders. Russia, and the eastern bloc communist countries guarded their international borders with the capitalist western countries zealously. East Berlin was barricaded with concrete walls, barbed wire concertina coils, with a string of sentry towers with powerful searchlights against the free city of West Berlin. The journalistic term "sealed the border" made sense only under these extreme conditions.

The borders with West and East Pakistan, guarded by State Armed Police Battalions remained quite soft from 1947 to 1965. There were a handful of Battalions with each of the Border States. There was not even a standard laid down of what should be an ideal inter Border Out Post (B.O.P.) distance. Then in 1965, Pakistan suddenly attacked and overran the Sardar post of the Kutch I.B. This ultimately led to the 1965 war with Pakistan and the Tashkent agreement. The Home Ministry then decided to raise the Border Security Force (B.S.F.) whose primary task it was to guard the I.B. with Pakistan, both in the West and in the East. The whole concept of border guarding changed with the B.S.F. taking over. There was now no shortage of funds. Several items became standardised. The Force was divided into Frontiers and Sectors. Starting with just 50 Battalions, the Force expanded to 157 by 1997. Till 1984, the borders however, continued to be soft, despite the Centre deploying one Force. The resort to terrorism by underground groups in Punjab changed the concept of border policing in India. The Punjab border with Pakistan was till that time, the border with the highest figures of gold being smuggled through a land border. The pay offs from this smuggling ran to crores of rupees and it was a well-known fact that the shares went right up to the highest officials in the State's hierarchy. The B.S.F. was also tarnished in the process and got its epithet Border Smuggling Force from its activities in Punjab, West Bengal, Assam and Tripura. When the terrorist groups in Punjab decided to take to arms, they crossed the I.B. into Pakistan. Just at that time Gen. Zia-ul-Haque was planning to train Kashmiri youths and infiltrate them into Jammu and Kashmir to start an insurgency there. The Russians had just withdrawn from Afghanistan and the Pakistan Inter Services Intelligence (I.S.I.) was flush with arms and only wanted manpower from Kashmir to be trained. It was at this precise moment that the Khalistanis walked into their arms. The I.S.I. quickly adjusted to this God-sent chance to subvert India and began arming and training the different Khalistani groups, and infiltrating them into India, with weapons and explosives. It was when this deadly infiltration started that the Home Ministry decided to fence and light the border. The task was taken up on a war footing and within one year the fence and lighting was completed. Acquisition of land was done after the fencing was completed. With the construction of the fence and lighting of the border a new concept of zero tolerance of infiltration was born. The B.S.F. now found that the officers and men on the spot were liable if the fence was cut and some one had crossed. Earlier when a crossing took place, they could always say that their ambush was in place but the infiltration took place elsewhere. Punjab, after the fence, got sufficient troops to reduce the inter B.O.P. distance to 2 kilometres, with a majority of B.O.P.s having a company strength. The result was there for everyone to see. Smuggling dropped by 90 per cent. By this time gold imports had been allowed, but heroin from Afghanistan was the hot item for smuggling. The profits were ten times more than for gold. The fence, however, was a major dampener. Attempts were made to dig tunnels under the fence, fix rendezvous by international calls and throwing the packets across. The border was however not porous, and more often than not it was human weakness leading to collusion that led to instances of smuggling. The human factor is common, but with the fence and lighting Force personnel who succumbed to temptation were also easily caught.

The fencing was extended to Rajasthan. Here in

Jaisalmer and Barmer, the border population of Muslims had relations across and movement was common across the I.B. In fact very often marriages took place across the I.B. With the construction of the fence and lighting of the border, all movement across the borders ceased. Seeing that the fence was effective on the Western Border, the B.S.F. asked for its weak underbelly, the West Bengal border to be fenced. Unfortunately the Home Ministry sanctioned only 400 odd kilometres of a 1,600 land border to be fenced. This was wrong from conception. If a border was to be fenced, all of it had to be fenced or nothing was to be fenced. There was no sense in fencing 400 odd kilometres in several different patches. Fortunately a project to construct a border road was simultaneously taken up for West Bengal, Assam and Meghalaya. Unfortunately the West Bengal Government from the beginning was not too happy with the construction of the fence. Acquisition of land was slow. The quality of the fencing was not as good as the fence in the Punjab. The border road was constructed on an embankment, but the fencing was constructed level with the ground. The whole of West Bengal is low lying. The 1,400 odd kilometres of land border is inundated for varying periods of 3 to 9 months of the year. In fact about 200 kilometres is under water throughout the year. It is not possible to police the border ahead and behind the fencing if it is inundated. This crucial factor was not thought of at the time of constructing the fencing. Obviously the fencing should have been erected on the bund constructed for the border road. These shortcomings have been pointed out to the government and it is hoped that changes will be implemented to make the fence foolproof as in the Western border.

West Bengal

The International Border (I.B.) with Bangladesh is 4,095 kilometres long and covers five states of India. The border with West Bengal is 2,217 kilometres, of which 600 kilometres are riverine, 200 kilometres low lying, generally under water and the remaining 1,417 kilometres on low land which is inundated for part of the year during the monsoon. The problems of policing the borders are compounded by the nature of the terrain, the hostile border population and the non-cooperation of the State Government and the general apathy of the Central Government to problems of the East. The international boundary starts at the mouth of the Harbhanga, one of a chain of interlocking streams that constitute the ecosystem of the Sunderbans. The I.B. runs along the midstream of the navigable channels. From the mouth of the Harbhanga you have to sail upstream for more than 50 kilometres before the first village is sighted. The reason why there is no habitation up to this point is because there is no fresh water. Tubewells yield only brackish water. The last post of the Border Security Force (B.S.F.) Shanshernagar is located here. Beyond this point, till the stream opens up before joining the sea, only stray fishing boats are seen. All the boats are of Bangladesh. Indian boats seldom venture beyond Shamshernagar because the B.S.F. patrols are rare. When the B.S.F. sends its patrol boats everything looks orderly, with the Bangladesh boats keeping to their side of the river. When there is no B.S.F. patrol, the Bangladesh fishermen generally plunder the catch of the Indian fishermen. The Indian fishermen therefore generally keep to the interior channels beyond Shamshernagar. The plan was to build medium craft and position them as floating

Border Out Posts (B.O.P.s) from Shamshernagar up to the mouth of the Harbhanga with smaller patrol craft with each medium craft so that the stretch from Shamshernagar to the mouth of the Harbhanga is policed. The medium craft are I believe about to be commissioned. For the last fifty odd years the stretch from Shamshernagar to the mouth of the Harbhanga has been an open border save for an odd patrol or two chugging up in an ancient medium craft.

From the first village near the Shamshernagar post of the B.S.F. virtually all the villages situated along the I.B. are involved in smuggling essential commodities to Bangladesh. The economy of the entire I.B. is based on this smuggling. In the towns located well behind the I.B. sit the mahajans who are the financiers and kingpins of the smuggling syndicates. It is they who arrange the commodities to be smuggled across—sugar, rice, mustard oil, cheap cloth and specially manufactured high alcohol content Phensydyl cough syrup. The poor inhabitants of the border villages are the couriers who actually carry the goods in bundles across. It is the mahajans who bribe the Customs and the B.S.F. and the Police. The ones who are caught are the poor villagers with their bundles of essential commodities. The mahajans who sit behind and control the finances are never caught. Upstream from Shamshernagar, the habitations increase in density on either bank until you hit the land border at boundary pillar No. 1 at Goalpara B.O.P. From here the border is thickly populated right up to the zero line till we cross into Assam. The density of population is particularly high in south Bengal. In West Bengal there are more than a hundred villages that are located right up to the zero line. In many villages there are houses where the front door is in India and the rear door opens into Bangladesh. Hilli town in Malda district is also located right on the border. A row of houses in this town have their front doors in India and their rear doors open on to the railway platform of Hilli in Bangladesh. Over the years continual migration of both Hindus and Muslims from Bangladesh has completely changed the demography of the border districts in south Bengal. The border belt in South 24 Parghanas, Nadia, Murshidabad, Malda and West Dinajpur up to varying depths of one to five kilometres is predominantly constituted by illegal settlers from Bangladesh. The Hindus and Muslims have invariably settled in homogeneous groups.

In 1947, very few Muslims from Assam and West Bengal migrated en masse to East Pakistan after partition, unlike in the west, where there was mass migration of Hindus and Sikhs from Pakistan to India and of Muslims from Punjab to Pakistan. Two things happened after partition in the eastern frontier. There were severe communal riots in East Pakistan in 1954 and 1963. On both occasions the Hindu and Buddhist communities were targeted and they migrated in thousands to India. They were settled in refugee camps and resettled later. Many who had migrated settled in West Bengal in the border districts. The second feature was the insidious migration of Muslims. This was basically for economic reasons. At first the State probably did not have a direct hand in this. The ruling elite of West Pakistan from the beginning neglected East Pakistan. There were existent populations of East Bengalis in several districts of Assam and West Bengal. The Muslim population of Cachar, Hailakandi and Goalpara were all Bengali Muslims who had migrated during the

British days. Karimganj was a subdivision of Sylhet district, and was given to India by Radcliffe. No one knows why, because it had a majority Muslim population. The quiet flow of Bengali Muslim population from East Pakistan to India started soon after partition. The districts of East Pakistan were already over populated. Holdings were small and earnings meagre. Daily wages for labour were higher in India and the Taka was poorer than the Rupee. It was natural for border villagers and town's people to cross the border, work for the day in India and return in the evenings to East Pakistan. Many of these itinerant workers quietly settled down in India in the border areas and then later started moving to the hinterland, as space became an increasingly scarce commodity. There is an interesting sidelight to this migration. Both in Assam and in West Bengal there are tribal populations. In West Bengal there are some Rajbongshi villages along the border from Cooch Bihar to Malda. Wherever these villages exist no migration of east Bengali Muslims has taken place. They have not allowed any settlements to take place either. The scenario in Meghalaya is even more interesting. The I.B. crosses over into Meghalaya, a little ahead of Mancachar. It is still a plains area. Bengali Muslims had settled in two plain areas of Phulbari and Mahendraganj during the British days when Garo Hills was a district of Assam. Beyond Mahendraganj, the border is the foothills of the Garo Hills, Khasi Hills and the Jaintia Hills, for more than 400 kilometres till the I.B. crosses over to Cachar district of Assam. The population is of Garos, Langams, Khasis and Jaintias in that order. There is not a single settlement of Bengali Muslims in this whole stretch. The local tribals neither allow migration nor settlement, though they regularly allow Bengali Muslim labour to come from across to work in their betel nut and orange plantations during the day. It is also of interest that there is hardly any intermarriage between Rajbongshis, Boros and all the hill tribals of Meghalaya with the Bengali Muslims.

The attitude of the West Bengal Government was very negative when the issue of fencing the border was taken up. Once when the Director General of the B.S.F. met the Chief Secretary in 1996 and told him of the continual infiltration of Bangladesh nationals into West Bengal, he observed that there was no difference between the proletariat of Bangladesh and the proletariat of West Bengal! Construction of the 400 odd kilometres of fencing originally sanctioned was held up for non-acquisition of land. There was very little help from the State Government. Where the fence was being constructed, there was the problem of nearly 100 odd villages located ahead of the alignment of the fencing. The State Government gave no help in re-siting the villages behind the alignment of the fencing. Interestingly in a whole stretch from Islampur to Malda, all the Hindu villages shifted their thatched houses themselves to land behind the alignment of the fencing, converting their erstwhile homestead land to paddy fields. Not a single Muslim village shifted. Foolishly the fence was constructed leaving the village ahead of the fence, a totally absurd situation.

In the stretch from Siliguri southwards, the Tea Companies were trying to extend tea cultivation. They found the land ahead of the fencing an attractive proposition. Local farmers were not happy with the strips of land ahead of the fencing and the gates in the fencing being closed at night and began selling the strips of land to the Tea Companies.

The B.S.F. found this a tactically useful proposition, and encouraged the Tea Companies to buy up the land ahead of the fencing and plant tea bushes there. They were told not to allow any habitation on the land ahead of the fence. The Bangladesh Rifles were most unhappy with this development and protested that tea should not be planted on the land ahead of the fencing, and even fired on our personnel. The B.S.F. took a firm stand and informed their counterparts that we would plant what we liked on our side. The whole axis where tea bushes were planted ahead of the fencing became easy for guarding and patrolling as there was no human habitation ahead of the fencing and it became a secure area. Smuggling and infiltration dropped to nil in these areas.

Except where stretches of fencing exists, and there is no habitation ahead of the fencing, the border is quite porous. Smuggling and infiltration is ubiquitous. The worst areas are in South and Central West Bengal. A whole hospital and Nursing Home industry has sprung up in the towns close to the Bangladesh borders. These cater exclusively for patients from Bangladesh. Some patients come with passports; the majority does not take the trouble to make passports. The border belt of West Bengal up to varying depths of one to five kilometres is now solidly Bangladeshi. The majority of these illegal migrants live on encroached land. The embankments of the Farakkha canals are solidly encroached for miles near Murshidabad. This whole migrant population has no means of livelihood but working as couriers for the mahajans of the smuggling trade.

With West Bengal at saturation point, illegal migrants from Bangladesh pass through and colonise vacant spaces in urban environments in Delhi, Mumbai, and Hyderabad. There are more than 10 lakh illegal Bangladeshi migrants across the Jamuna in Delhi, with their unofficial transit camp at Nizamuddin. Along with the constant movement to and fro, slip in cadres of the Harkat-ul-Jihad-e-Islami (H.U.J.I.), Harkat-ul-Mujahideen (H.U.M.) and related Muslim fundamentalist groups. While there is no large-scale infiltration with weapons and explosives as across the Line of Control from Pakistan-occupied Kashmir or through the I.B. in Meghalaya and Tripura, small groups with arms and explosives do slip in through the Bengal border to commit specific acts of sabotage. Senior and middle-level leaders of militant groups of the Harkat-ul-Ansar (H.U.A.), Harkat-ul-Jihad-Islami (H.U.J.I.) and Lashkar-e-Taiba (L.E.T.) enter and exit through the Bangladesh border. Once in 1995, on specific information from an Intelligence agency, a search was conducted at an Islamic institution in Deoband, to detect militants suspected to be sheltering there. This was considered an affront to the Muslim community, and the officials were almost suspended. Just a fortnight after this, a leading member of the H.U.A., a Pakistani was caught by the B.S.F. when trying to slip into Bangladesh. On interrogation, he confessed that he had come from Kashmir and was trying to slip into Bangladesh, from where he would go to Pakistan. En route he had sheltered at the same religious institution in Deoband. There are several instances of Pakistanis members of militant groups who have been intercepted while trying to infiltrate or exfiltrate at the Bangladesh borders.

The I.B. in North Bengal is only slightly less porous than South Bengal as regards infiltration of civilian population.

There is however frequent crossing by cadres of the United Liberation Front of Assam (U.L.F.A.), National Democratic Front of Bodoland (N.D.F.B.) and the Kamtapur Liberation Organisation (K.L.O.), from their camps in Bhutan, located just north and east of the Sankoch River, the boundary between West Bengal and Assam. The K.L.O. is an organisation of the Rajbongshis of Bengal, who are unhappy with the treatment given to them by the caste Hindus of Bengal.

Assam-Dhubri District

The I.B. in Assam's Dhubri district is 134 kilometres. The stretch from the Cooch Bihar border to the Brahmaputra is fenced; the last 20 kilometres have been washed away in floods. Except for a few very old Rajbongshi villages, Chatrasal and Ramraikuti all the border villages are of immigrant Muslims. These villages are sanctuaries for illegal migrants. U.L.F.A. cadres use the Rajbongshi villages for crossing. Then comes the Brahmaputra. The river curves at this point and the I.B. is more than 15 kilometres long along the river. There are seven B.O.P.s, all temporary located on islands called chars. These chars are formed and reformed with each flood. In a flood a whole char may disappear and reform elsewhere in a new shape. The chars are inhabited exclusively by immigrant Muslims. This stretch of the I.B. is a weak link for the B.S.F. It is not difficult to slip through on dark nights taking shelter in the chars to avoid the patrol boats of the B.S.F. On the south bank, from Hallidayganj to Mancachar is a solid belt of immigrant Muslims. The border is fenced but the land is low-lying and dozens of nullahs flow into the Brahmaputra. These are natural gaps in the fencing. The population is also supportive of the infiltrators.

Meghalaya

Beyond Mancachar, the I.B. enters Meghalaya. The border initially runs in the plains. Immigrant Muslims thickly inhabit two Police Station areas, Mahendraganj and Phulbari. These were migrants who came in during the British days. This is a porous border for migration of civilians. Shelter is always available from the friendly population. Beyond this area the I.B. runs along the foothills of the Garo, Khasi and Jaintia hills for the rest of the 443 kilometres. The terrain is thickly forested with elephants wandering on to the lonely border road at night. The Indian side is replete with timber, coal and limestone. Across in Bangladesh, there are hardly any trees. There are of course no stones, no limestone and no coal. Groups of Bangladeshis move up the fast flowing streams in the rainy season and rowing expertly upstream, cut trees from the forests and float them down to Bangladesh. The B.S.F. is stretched thinly along this border with the inter B.O.P. distance being 6 to 8 kilometres. The Observation Parties detailed are often of 2 or 3 men. The raiding parties from Bangladesh are of groups of 10 to 15 men armed with daos and spears. When challenged by the B.S.F. patrols, they do not hesitate to attack them. The B.S.F.patrol have naturally to fire at them. When complaining to our High Commissioner in Dacca, the Bangladesh officials state that the B.S.F. fired at innocent grass cutters. They forget to mention that the trespassers were after trees, not grass. As mentioned earlier, the Garo, Khasi and Jaintia landowners regularly engage Bangladeshi labour in their orange and betel nut orchards. They, however, never allow them to settle on their land. There is thus no infiltration of civilians along this whole axis. The tribal mahajans however have a very good understanding with their counterpart traders in Bangladesh and there is a flourishing illegal trade in the small border towns like Dawki, Muktapur, Nayabazaar, Lynkhat, Bholaganj, Shella, Rengku, Balaat, Dalu and Baghmara. These small towns located right on the border are inaccessible and far from the prying eyes of senior officers of the Customs and the B.S.F. and this thriving trade flourishes quietly. In fact it is the livelihood for the poor people of these remote border towns.

Cadres of the Garo and Khasi insurgent groups, the Achik National Volunteer Council (A.N.V.C.) and the Hynniewtrep National Liberation Council (H.N.L.C.) use the whole border from Dalu in the west to Ratacherra in the east to cross over into Bangladesh and bring back arms. It is also used by the N.D.F.B. and the U.L.F.A. for the same purpose. The National Socialist Council of Nagaland (N.S.C.N.) also uses the border particularly from Dawki eastwards for crossing into Bangladesh. Unfortunately, the border road and the fencing in part of Khasi Hills, from Maheshkolla to Balaat has not been properly aligned. The fencing should have been constructed parallel to the border and the border road parallel to the fencing a 100 yards behind. The fencing and the border road keep crossing and recrossing and we have an absurd situation of openings in the fencing where the border road crosses and recrosses it. This was pointed out to the Government and hopefully is being rectified. The quantum of troops in this sector has to be increased to make the inter B.O.P. distance 2 to 3 kilometres and to have a minimum strength of 2 platoons in each B.O.P. With properly aligned fencing and sufficient strength, this border can be effectively policed to prevent any crossing.

Assam-Cachar and Karimganj Districts

From Ratacherra, the easternmost point of the I.B. in Meghalaya, the border turns south and for 134 kilometres runs along the Cachar and Karimganj districts of Assam. The border population consists of Bengali Hindus and Muslims. More than half the border is along the banks of the Kushiara and the Surma rivers. The whole of Cachar and Karimganj is thickly populated and villages are sited right upto the banks of these two rivers. The actual border is the middle of the navigable stream. In the winter the two streams for most of its length become quite shallow and people can cross on foot. It is impossible to police this border until the villages are resited at least 150 yards from the floodwater mark of the two rivers and all navigation by boats is strictly controlled from specified ghats. Further south, the terrain changes to thickly wooded country, interspersed with the characteristic tillas of the Chittagong Hill Tracts (C.H.T.). These are small hillocks with nullahs inbetween. Karimganj district was a subdivision of the erstwhile Sylhet district of East Bengal and was wrongly given to Assam by Radcliffe. The population is mainly Bengali Muslim. Over the years the Jamait-e-Ulema-e Islam has spread its roots among the Muslim population of the district. This sect of Islam controls almost all the mosques along the border. It must be remembered that the H.U.A. and the H.U.J.I. are terrorist groups of this fundamentalist sect of Islam. It is not surprising therefore that infiltration of cadres of these two terrorist groups has taken place frequently through this border. North of Karimganj, there are a number of Manipuri Meithei villages, remnants of the incursions of the Manipuri Rajas into Cachar and East Bengal. These villages provide shelter to cadres of the People's Liberation Army (P.L.A.) and the United National Liberation Front (U.N.L.F.) insurgent groups of Manipur, while crossing over into Bangladesh. This is also a very big axis for smuggling. The kingpins are the Marwari traders of Karimganj. Their godowns abut on the Kushiara River. Every village teems with couriers whose small boats, carrying smuggled goods, keep dodging the B.S.F.patrol boats. In all senses this is a very sensitive border and it is absolutely necessary to resite all villages and towns from the riverbanks of the Kushiara and the Surma and create a security zone from the high flood mark to the water level. Fencing is yet to be completed on this border and it must be done as suggested if this border has to be controlled.

Tripura

By the time the border enters Tripura, the terrain has changed to thickly forested hills and populated valleys. Tripura has a border of 856 kilometres. There are six, roughly north- south ranges—Deotamura, Baramura, Atharimura, Langtrai, Sakhan and Jampui. There are also a number of east-west ranges, which link the main north-south ranges. In between are verdant valleys. The plain areas are inhabited by Bengali Hindus and some Muslims, all migrants from East Bengal. The hills are exclusively the domain of the indigenous tribals—Dev Barmans, Tripuris, Jamatiyas, Riangs and Chakmas. The majority of the Hindu and Muslim Bengalis migrated to Tripura after partition. The ruling raja had himself invited Hindu Bengalis to come and settle in Tripura even before the British came as the East India Company. However the population of Bengali Hindus and Muslims before partition was only about 20 per cent of the tribals. It is the wave of migration after partition that has upset the demographic balance. Today the Bengali Hindus and Muslims are nearly 70 per cent, while the tribals are only 30 per cent. To compound the problem, all the plain land has passed into the hands of the Bengali Hindus and Muslims, and the tribals have been pushed into the hinterland. Among the tribal groups, the Chakmas have migrated from the C.H.T. Today the small Chakma population lives in the remote inaccessible hills of south and east Tripura along the border of the C.H.T. Most of their villages are accessible only after two or three days march. There are two tribal insurgent groups, the National Liberation Front of Tripura (N.L.F.T.) and the All Tripura Tiger Force (A.T.T.F.) fighting for independence. Both the groups have camps in Bangladesh, mainly in the C.H.T. and also in Srimangal district to the north. We have enough evidence from interrogation reports and source information that the Bangladesh Directorate of Forces Intelligence (D.G.F.I.), and the Bangladesh Rifles (B.D.R.) have helped these two groups to establish their training camps. The N.S.C.N. (I.M.) has helped both groups to purchase arms with the help of the I.S.I. of Pakistan from the arms bazaar of Thailand. The N.S.C.N. has also helped in training the cadres. The main problem of tackling this insurgency is the long porous border of Tripura. The groups freely enter from their sanctuaries in the north, in Srimangal district of Bangladesh, along the thickly forested slopes of the Deotamura, Baramura and the Atharimura ranges that originate in Bangladesh and traverse into Tripura. In the south, the groups slip into Tripura from the C.H.T. along the slopes of the Langtrai, Sakhan and Jampui ranges. The B.S.F. do not have enough battalions to have an inter B.O.P.

distance of 2 kilometres with at least one company in each B.O.P. which is the minimum required to prevent infiltration. The border fencing has just been taken up while the border road has yet to be constructed in the most sensitive portions from S.K. Para to Kanthlang, the trijunction of the C.H.T., Tripura and Mizoram. Most of the B.O.P.s along the C.H.T. on the forested slopes of the Deotamura, Baramura and the Atharimura ranges are 5 to 6 kilometres apart and have a strength of only one platoon. The N.L.F.T. and A.T.T.F. parties easily bypass the posts and slip in, hit their targets of kidnapping local leaders or killing Bengali Hindus and then slip back into the safety of Bangladesh. When constructing the border fence, care must be taken to construct it parallel to the border road. The present number of B.O.P.s must be tripled, so that there is a maximum inter B.O.P. distance of 2 kilometres. The strength of each B.O.P. should be kept at one company. Only then is it possible to deploy ambushes to deter insurgent groups from slipping in. Along the western borders of Tripura, the terrain is mostly plain with interspersing tillas. There are a large number of villages located along the zero line, with some houses straddling the border. The scenario is a repetition of West Bengal, with the village population all functioning as couriers, the mahajans located in the towns near the border supplying sugar, mustard oil, rice and cheap cloth. A lot of timber is also smuggled. While the essential commodities are all smuggled by the Bengali Hindu and Muslim community, the tribals are engaged in timber smuggling. Trees are cut in the forests bordering the C.H.T. and thrown into the Feni river. When one looks across into Bangladesh from Katalcherra B.O.P. in South Tripura a large number of saw mills are seen busily working, the raw material obviously coming from Tripura.

Mizoram

The last stretch of the I.B. with Bangladesh starts from the trijunction of the C.H.T., Tripura and Mizoram and ends at the tri junction of the C.H.T., Mizoram and Myanmar at Parva. The distance between these two trijunctions is 318 kilometres and there is only one battalion guarding this stretch. The inter B.O.P. distance varies from 20 to 25 kilometres. Obviously very little border guarding can be done with this strength. Each B.O.P. can only sanitise the area around it. The N.S.C.N. (I.M.) went to Bangladesh in 1990 and linked up with the I.S.I., who arranged for purchase of arms from Thailand. These were brought by tramp steamers to Cox's Bazaar, collected and taken overland to Bandarban, Parva and then along the southern and eastern border of Mizoram into Churachandpur district of Manipur and then via Tamenglong to Nagaland. Three such consignments were taken by the N.S.C.N. The Indian Army with the help of the Myanmar Army ambushed the fourth consignment. Cadres of the N.S.C.N. (I.M.), U.L.F.A. and the N.D.F.B.were killed, 58 in all and 40 were captured and a sizeable number of arms seized. After this the N.S.C.N changed its strategy and changed the incoming route. From Bandarban, the group ferrying the arms struck north and traversing the C.H.T. slipped into Mizoram between the last post of the.B.S.F. at Kanthlang and the first post at Tuipuibari entering the Longai valley. Going further south along this valley, the group would veer east and traversing Mizoram reach Tipaimukh in the eastern tip of Churachandpur district of Manipur. From here the group would strike north on the Man Bahadur road and crossing N.H. 53 reach Tamenglong district and then into Nagaland. The only way to stop this movement is to fortify this stretch of the border. The N.S.C.N. (I.M.) now have a camp in Aizawl, and it is learnt that the last two consignments of arms collected from Cox's Bazaar and brought via Bandarban, Tuipuibari to the Longai valley was received by an N.S.C.N. party and the arms transferred to vehicles and taken via Silchar on the Aizawl Silchar highway and then via Jiribam to Tamenglong and then to Nagaland. Some nexus appears to have been developed between the party in power in Mizoram and the N.S.C.N. (I.M.). Very obviously the strength of the force on the Mizoram border has to be increased to achieve an inter B.O.P.distance of 2 kilometres, with each B.O.P. having a company strength.

The Threat from Bangladesh

There is a continuous flow of people from Bangladesh into India. This flow is for economic reasons as far as the Bengali Muslims are concerned. Besides this there is also a continuous flow of Bengali Hindus and Buddhists into India. This is because of State sponsored acts of terrorism on the minority population. Bangladesh refuses to publish figures of its minority population. It is probably about 10 lakhs today down from a figure of 60 lakhs in 1977. Knowing the ground conditions in Bangladesh, we should expect the remaining 10 lakhs to cross over. If they are being persecuted for their religion, we cannot refuse sanctuary to them. But that is not the end of the story. Side by side the flow of Bengali Muslims is only going to increase further. I quote from an article written by Sadiq Khan, an intellectual belonging to an illustrious and politically active family, published in *Holiday*, a weekly published from Dacca, titled "The Question of Lebensraum." [1] To quote: " The question of lebensraum or living space for the people of Bangladesh has not yet been raised as a moot issue. All projections indicate that by the next decade Bangladesh will face a serious crisis of lebensraum. No possible performance of population planning actual or hypothetical alters that prediction." The article goes on to suggest a world demographic order as an adjunct to the new international economic order, whereby population can be equitably distributed.to prevent critical demographic pressures in pockets of high concentration. In the event of such international cooperation not forthcoming, the author suggested the following: "A natural overflow of population pressure is therefore very much on the cards and will not be restrained by barbed wire or border patrol measures. The natural trend of population overflow from Bangladesh is towards the sparsely populated lands of the southeast in the Arakans and in the northeast of the seven sisters side of the Indian subcontinent. It is in this context that we must see the actions of the Bangladesh Government in refusing to reply to our queries during the process of consular access and their further actions of pushing their citizens who are pushed into Bangladesh back into India.

Ever since the foreigners' agitation, during which there were ethnic clashes between the Assamese and the immigrant Muslims in Goalpara, Kamrup, Nowgong and Darrang districts, Pakistan's I.S.I. and Bangladesh's D.G.F.I. have been funding and building up Muslim fundamentalist groups in Assam. The role of the D.G.F.I. was always underplayed. It is only recently that the role of the D.G.F.I. has been fully understood. The main Muslim groups that have come up are:

1. Muslim United Liberation Front of Assam. (M.U.L.F.A.)

2. Muslim United Liberation Tigers of Assam. (M.U.L.T.A.)

3. Islamic Liberation Army of Assam. (I.L.A.A.)

4. United Muslim Liberation Front of Assam. (U.M.F.L.A.)

5. Peoples United Liberation Front. (P.U.L.F.)

6. Muslim Volunteer Force. (M.V.F.)

7. Adam Sena.

Besides these, the H.U.M and the H.U.J.I. have been operating since 1990-92. Details of the data obtained by Assam Police on the activities of the I.S.I. and the different Muslim groups, were laid on the table of the Assam assembly by the Chief Minister of Assam on April 6, 2000.[2] This document clearly details the U.L.F.A. leaders regular movement to Pakistan from Bangladesh and of the training imparted to them in Mujahideen camps in Peshawar. Prior to this the Assam Police had arrested four persons on suspicion on August 10, 1999 in Gauhati. They turned out to be

1. Mohammed Fasiullah Hussaini alias Hamid Mohammed alias Khalid Mohammed of Hyderabad Sind Pakistan.

2. Md. Javed Wakhar alias Md. Musaffa alias Md. Mehraj alias Abdul Rehman Danish of Karachi Pakistan.

3. Maulana Hafiz Md. Akram Mallick alias Musaffar Husain of Mukaran Shahwali Kupwara Kashmir.

4. Qari Salim Ahmed alias Abdul Aziz of Mehilki Muzaffarnagar. U.P.

These people had arrived in Dacca via Karachi on

different dates and met I.S.I. officials in Dacca and crossed over into India through the Karimganj border. They had kept a consignment of explosives in a mosque in Bangladesh that was brought in by a clever operation using a decoy. The recovery consisted of 34 kgs. of R.D.X., 9 timer devices, and 30 detonators. During interrogation, the group disclosed that the H.U.M. had recruited and sent a number of young men for training to Pakistan via Bangladesh. Based on this information, the Assam Police was able to arrest a number of young men who had been trained in Pakistan and returned. They also arrested Mohammed Muslimudeen, the Chief organiser of the H.U.M. in Assam. They found that the Naib Amir of H.U.M. in India Maulana Md. Fakruddin alias Akram Master is from Goalpara and is now based in Pakistan. The role of the D.G.F.I. in all these transactions remains shadowy. Throughout they have been the go-betweens or intermediaries in the operations of the I.S.I. with the Northeastern militant groups.

The Al Qaeda Connection

Bangladesh over the past decade has gone through a fundamental political and social transformation. A new brand of nationalism with an Islamist flavour is gradually replacing secular Bengali nationalism. Besides, Intelligence organisations, local journalists and Non-Governmental organisations have managed to locate several training camps in the country, mainly in the lawless southeast bordering Myanmar.[3] Since the last general elections, Bangladesh is ruled by a coalition. The Jamaat-e-Islami (J.E.I.), who sided with Pakistan during the Freedom struggle, has 17 seats with two Ministers. The Jamaat's militants fought alongside the Pakistan army against the Bengali nationalists. Among the most notorious of the Jamaat's leaders was Abdul Khader Molla, who became known as the butcher of Mirpur. He fled to Pakistan and so could not be prosecuted as a war criminal. Today he has returned and is the Publicity Secretary of the Jamaat. The present coalition also includes a smaller but very virulent Islamic party, the Islamic Oikya Jote, whose Chairman Azizul Haque, is a member of the H.U.J.I. Council.

The Arakan area of Myanmar is separated from the rest of the country by a densely forested mountain range. The Burmese who lived in this tract remained isolated till the 9th century, when Moorish, Arab and Persian traders landed on their coast. Some of them intermarried. There was also migration from the thickly populated Chittagong coast into the Arakans. This mélange speaking mainly the Chittagong dialect of Bengali interspersed with Persian, Arabic and Arakanese came to be known as the Rohingyas. In 1978, the Myanmar Government launched an operation to check illegal migrants. Troops moved around the Arakans among the Rohingyas arresting people at random. More than 2 lakh Rohingyas migrated to Teknaf and Cox's Bazaar as refugees. There was an international outcry and many refugees did return, but thousands settled between Cox's Bazaar and Teknaf. Being good sailors many found employment in cargo ships and thus found their way to Karachi. A colony of Rohingyas came up in Karachi. It was about this time that the Pashtuns from the North West Frontier Province also settled in Karachi. The Pashtuns were all followers of the J.U.I. and many were jihad fighters in the H.U.J.I. and the H.U.M. The Rohingyas had a cause and back in Teknaf, the Rohingya Solidarity Organisation (R.S.O.) had been formed to fight in Myanmar. Camps to train the R.S.O. cadres came up near the Myanmar border. The link between the Rohingyas in Karachi and the H.U.M. and the H.U.J.I., there came in quite handy and many Rohingyas were sent for training to the Mujahdeen camps in Khost in Afghanistan. Afghan instructers came to train the R.S.O. cadres in their camps at Ukhia near Cox's Bazaar. The U.S. Army started operations in Afghanistan at the end of 2001. During these operations they recovered 60 videotapes from an Al Qaeda camp. One of them was marked Burma and showed cadres training in the camp. On verification it was found that the camp was in Ukhia and all the trainees were not Rohingyas. Some were members of the Islamic Chatra Shibir, the youth wing of the Jamaat of Bangladesh. It is learnt that this camp was taken over by the Bangladesh H.U.J.I. formed in 1992, allegedly with support from Osama bin Laden. H.U.J.I. has now more then 15,000 cadres. The group now known as the Bangladesh Taliban has become notorious for masterminding attacks on the Hindu minority and moderate Muslims in Bangladesh. In an interview with the C.N.N. in December 2001, the U.S. Taliban fighter John Walker Lindh mentioned that the Al Qaeda brigades to which he belonged was divided along linguistic lines into Arabic, Pakistani and Bengali. The Bengali group consisted mostly of Rohingyas, but also some Bangladeshis.[4]

It is now finally established that a ship the M.V.Mecca sailed from Karachi in late November or December 2001 and anchored on a sand bank 3 kilometres out to sea from Chittagong port on the night of December 31, 2001. Seeing it anchor out at sea was a signal for the port workers not to ask any questions. Port workers that night said they saw five motor launches ferry in large groups of men, wearing traditional salwar kameez and black turbans, with long beards. Their towering heights suggested that these travellers were foreigners and the AK 47s slung across their shoulders gave them away. Then in July 2002, a senior member of the Bangladesh H.U.J.I. informed *Time* that the 150 men who landed at Chittagong on that night were Taliban and Al Qaeda fighters from Afghanistan. This was confirmed by other sources from the Bangladesh Army. On October 7, 2002, the Indian Police arrested one Fazle Karim, alias Abu Fuji in Calcutta as he arrived by train from Kashmir on his way to Bangladesh. A veteran of Al Qaeda camps in eastern Afghanistan, he told his interrogators that he had twice met Bin Laden and he recognised two fighters with whom he had trained in Afghanistan while visiting H.U.J.I. hideouts in Bangladesh in August 2002. The pair told him that they were part of a group of 100 Arabs and Afghans who had come by ship to Chittagong in winter. On September 24, 2002, Bangladesh's domestic intelligence agency arrested 4 Yemenis, an Algerian, a Lebanese and a Sudanese in the upper crust district of Uttara in Dacca. They found that the men were involved in arms training in a madrassa in Dacca, run by a Saudi-based charity Al Haramein. All the men were later taken to court and released. From the court they were taken to the Sheraton, from where they disappeared. A H.U.J.I. source confirmed that these men were from the M.V. Mecca.[5] It is also confirmed by sources from the Bangladesh H.U.J.I. and port workers, that the man who received the Taliban fighters from the M.V. Mecca on December 21, 2001 was a Major from the D.G.F.I. The H.U.J.I. and a Bangladesh military source confirmed that the Major was the last link in an operation that began in Afghanistan. Between May 10-11, 2002, nine fundamentalist groups in

Bangladesh met at a camp near Ukhia and formed the Bangladesh Islamic Manch. The new organisation includes the R.S.O. and the M.U.L.T.A.

Bangladesh is no longer a moderate Muslim country. The triple threat of continuous demographic assault, assistance and shelter to more than a dozen insurgent groups from the Northeast and the launching of fundamentalist militants from Pakistan through the Bangladesh border now hangs menacingly over our country. We have never given importance to the Bangladesh border as we have given to our western borders. Further neglect will be playing into our enemies' hands. The clear nexus between the Pakistan I.S.I. and the Bangladesh D.G.F.I. means that there is now no difference between the Pakistan and Bangladesh borders. In fact because of the density of the population on the Bangladesh borders, and its composition in West Bengal, Assam and parts of Tripura, this border is much more difficult to police than the western border. The Government must take the following steps immediately:

1. Create a clear security zone of 100 to 150 yards along the whole Bangladesh border, by resiting all villages and towns presently located right upto the zero line.

2. Construct border fencing on every foot of the land border, if necessary by building an embankment in low-lying areas

3. Ensure that the fencing is parallel to the border road and ahead of it. Where necessary this has to be rectified where it has been wrongly aligned.

4 Install lights along the border, as in the west.

5. The strength of the B.S.F. on the eastern border to be increased so that the inter B.O.P. distance is brought to 2 kilometres. The strength of each B.O.P. should be one company.

6. In the riverine borders, floating B.O.Ps should be positioned with smaller armed patrol boats with each mother craft so that every foot of the water channel that forms the border is covered.

It is only if these measures are taken that we will be able to defeat the three-pronged attack from Bangladesh. The nation has had enough indications of the threat from what was felt to be a friendly neighbour.

References

1. Sadiq Khan. "The Question of Lebensraum", *Holiday,* Dacca, October 18, 1991.

2. I.S.I. activities in Assam. Statement laid on the table of the house of the Assam Legislative Assembly under item No. 12 dated April 6, 2000 by the Chief Minister of Assam.

3. Bertil Lintner. "Bangladesh Extremist Islamic Consolidation", *Faultlines,* Vol. 14.

4. Transcript of John Walker interview. C.N.N., July 4, 2002.

5. *Time*. "Deadly Cargo." October 21, 2002.

The Naga Insurgency

The Naga insurgency is the oldest insurgency of independent India. Gestating from the run up to independence, it erupted in 1955-56, leading to enactment of the harsh Assam Disturbed Areas act and the Armed Forces Special Powers Act, and the first move by an insurgent group to a foreign country to seek help to fight the government. The insurgency was quite fierce, and necessitated the deployment of the army, first a brigade strength, later a division. The 8th mountain division earned its spurs in fighting this insurgency, and had built up an excellent reputation for its knowledge of the area and its peoples. Many illustrious generals commanded this division in Nagaland, and when it was shifted to Kashmir in the early 1990s, many old Naga hands, felt that it was not a correct decision. The Assam Rifles took over the responsibility for this sector, and though they have done well, have never been able to attain the charisma, which the 8th mountain division had built up.

There is a whole literature on the Naga insurgency, written over the years by army, intelligence bureau, civilian officers who worked or operated in the area, and by a number of academics, all Nagas. A number of myths have developed about this insurgency during this period. Why did this insurgency develop, and why has it continued for so long, though with a break in 1975 when an accord was signed with a faction, and will it now finally end?

The Nagas consist of about 30 odd tribes who inhabit

the present Nagaland state, parts of Manipur, a small part of North Cachar hills and Karbi Anglong in Assam, and a part of the old Tirap district of Arunachal Pradesh. The Naga leadership and historians claim that several small tribes in Manipur and Arunachal Pradesh are Naga, but this is disputed by the Chin-Kuki-Mizo leaders who claim that these were really Kuki tribes who have decided to be Naga because the Naga insurgent group is more powerful and it helps to be with the stronger group. There are several Naga tribes who live in Myanmar in the Sagaing Division opposite Nagaland and in the Somrah tracts, opposite Manipur. These are however the same tribes who live on the Indian side. In Nagaland the main tribes are the Angami, Ao, Sema, Konyak, Lotha, Chakesang, Rengma, Pochuri, Sangtam, Yimchunger, Khiamnungan, Phom and Zeliangrong, the last a group of three tribes, the Rongmei, Liangmei and Zemi. In Manipur, the Nagas dominate three districts. Ukhrul is the home of the Thangkuls, Senapati of the Maos, Marams, Poumeis and a very small tribe the Thengals and Tamenglong is dominated by the Zeliangrong. Chandel is divided between several Naga and Kuki tribes. The Kuki leaders claim that several tribes, whom the Naga leadership claims to be Naga, are really Kuki. These are the Maring, Anal, Lamkhang, Moyon, Monsong, Chote, Chiru and Tarao.[1] In Assam, in the North Cachar hills, there are a number of villages of Zemis, a minority compared to the Dimasa Cachari who dominate the district and the Kukis and Hmars, who are in a sizeable majority. In Myanmar, the Thangkuls live in the Somrah tracts opposite Ukhrul district, while in the Sagaing division opposite Nagaland are the Konyak, Phom, Yimchunger, and several smaller tribes. Three tribes in the old Tirap district are Naga.

Who are the Nagas and what is their origin? There is an aura of mystery about the origin of the Nagas, and their migration to their present habitation in Nagaland, Manipur, and the districts of Khonsa and Changlang of Arunachal Pradesh, and in Myanmar. There are no composite 'Naga' people, and among them there are many distinct tribes having more than 30 dialects, with every tribe constituting a separate language group. Their cultural and social setup varies vastly from tribe to tribe. Their physique and appearance differ from group to group. The nomenclature 'Naga' was given to this group by outsiders. In fact, for long the appellation of 'Naga' was resented, till political expediency caused it to be accepted. The different tribes, which constitute the Naga people, are rigidly distinct from one another. In many cases these tribes existed in complete isolation.[2] In fact the different Naga tribes never ever lived as one group.

For the majority of tribes, the entity was the village, and each village was independent of each other. There were both Monarchical and Republican systems in each village. Among the lower Konyaks and the Maos, some sort of confederation was found where the great kings act as the titular head over some other villages. The Angs, the kings of Konyak villages, used to pay tribute to the great Ang, who had however no power to interfere with the other Angs.[3] Among the Aos, Tatars (Councillors), who were the representatives of the people, could become the chief of the village by way of one's merit. In general, a Naga village was said to be self-sufficient, and by and large, maintained its sovereignty. Any interference, trespassing or encroachment by members of other villages in its territorial jurisdiction usually provoked inter-village war, where head hunting could follow.

It is generally held that the Ahoms were the first outsiders to come into contact with the Naga tribes. This is not correct. The first organised group who came into contact with the Naga tribes were the Meitheis. The Meitheis have a recorded history of nearly 2000 years, the Cheitharon Kumbaba. In his *My Experience in Manipur*, James Johnstone said, "The territories of Manipur varied according to the mettle of its rulers. Sometimes they held considerable territories east of the Chindwin River, at other times only the Kebaw valley." As for the north, "In 1835, indeed the forest between the Doyang and Dhansiri was declared to be the boundary between Manipur and Assam."[4] To quote further, "The Government was and still inclined to regard the Manipuris as the de facto master of the hills" (Naga Hills).[5] There are numerous references in the recorded history of Manipur, of relations with the Naga tribes, of tributes being paid by Naga tribal chiefs. There are also instances of Naga men being recruited in the army of the Manipuri kings. Many of the Naga tribes spoke the Meithei language. In 1878, the Chief Commissioner of Assam reported (Assam Proceedings, March 1878), that he considered Kohima the best site for the headquarters...and the Manipur frontier line. Even after compelling Manipur to cooperate with the British Government in bringing the Nagas under the subjection of British rule, Lt. Vincent showed that there were two parties in every Angami village, one attached to the interests of Manipur and another to that of the British. Johnson said in his *My Experience in Manipur*: "There is every reason to believe that Manipuris in former days did penetrate into the Naga Hills and exacted tribute when they felt strong enough to do so. All the villages have Manipuri names in addition to their own.... Whenever a Manipuri visited a Naga village, he was treated as an honoured guest, at a time when a British subject could not venture into the interior without risk of being murdered. Many of the Nagas spoke Manipuri, and several villages paid annual tribute."

The Ahoms came into contact with the Naga tribes, as they accosted them when they were migrating to Assam from the Shan area in Myanmar. The Naga tribes fiercely resisted the movement of the Ahoms through their territory. Later when the Ahoms settled in the Brahmaputra valley, and set up their Capital at Gurgaon in Sibsagar, there were several clashes with the Nagas over the collection of salt from the salt licks, which happened to lie in Naga territory. According to Verrier Elwin, the Ahom kings regarded the Nagas as their subjects and took taxes from them in the form of slaves, elephant tusks.[6]

The British came to the Northeast from East Bengal, as the East India Company. In fact they came to Manipur through Cachar, and then linked up with upper Assam through the Naga Hills. They soon set up tea gardens in the foothills, and that is when they encroached on the territory of Naga villages. Each Naga village was an entity and its lands were sacrosanct. Clashes took place and it was then that expeditions began to be sent into the Naga Hills. Areas bordering the plains had to be protected from the depredations of the hostile Nagas, who only wanted to be left alone. The British thus entered the Naga Hills and established posts inside so that the plains below could be protected. They also wanted their axis to Manipur from Golaghat to be safe. In January 1832, Captain Jenkins and Pemberton, led 800 Manipuri troops from the Manipur valley to Mohung Dijua on the Jamoona. This was probably some town on the bank of the Brahmaputra. In East Bengal the Brahmaputra was known as the Jamuna. They had to fight their way through the Zeliang and Angami Naga country. After several such skirmishes the East India Company decided to bring the Naga Hills directly under the British government. The British then organised a series of expeditions into the Naga Hills culminating in establishing the Naga Hills District at Samagooting (Chumukdima) in 1866, shifted to Kohima in 1878. Following the forward policy, the British were able to establish control over the whole of the Naga Hills. The policy of the British in administering the Naga Hills was one of defence and conciliation, not of coercion.[7] Enough autonomy and protection was given to the Nagas and all the hill people. The Inner Line Regulation is the best example of this. This was the first law promulgated in Assam under the authority conferred on the Government for summary legislation for backward tracts. This regulation was done to prevent friction between the hill and plains people. The Naga tribes were, by a Regulation of 1880, excluded from coming under such laws as may be complex or in any way unsuitable to them. The Governor General of India could, as laid down in the Government of India Act of 1919, proclaim any part of India to be a backward area. The word backward being objected to, it was decided to call all such areas excluded areas. Unwittingly the germs of separatism were laid with these two regulations, though they were passed with the best of intentions and for the good of the Nagas.

The Nagas were exposed to the outside world for the first time, during the First World War. About 2000 Nagas were recruited in the pioneer corps and served in France. Probably the first thoughts of Nagas as a complete group, struck these First World War veterans when they returned. They preferred to be under the direct administration of the British, so that their rights were protected and guarded against all encroachments from the non-Nagas.

At this stage a peculiar development took place in Tamenglong in Manipur, home of the Zeliangrong Nagas, comprising the Zemi, Liangmei and the Rongmei. A young man Jadonang, born in a Rongmei village, Kambiron grew up into a mystic and as he collected a following, began weeding out negative religious beliefs, which harmed his tribe. He began a social and religious reformation, which gradually turned to a movement against the British rule. Very soon the British had a minor revolt against some of their unfair practices in the form of civil disobedience, and a no tax campaign. During this period four Meitheis, itinerant traders, were killed in Kambiron village for insulting the religious sentiments of the Zeliang people. The British blamed Jadunong for the killings and arrested him and after a virtually mock trial hanged him. Gaidinliu of Nungkao village in Tamenglong was his lieutenant when Jadonang was hanged. She was just 16, but she resumed the fight. For a year she dodged the British, but was captured and imprisoned for life. She was released only a few years before independence. When the Naga insurgency broke out, she opposed it tooth and nail and had to go underground once again. She organised an army of nearly 1,000 men armed with rifles. There were several skirmishes between the underground Naga army and Gaidinliu's army. Her heroic efforts gradually fizzled out as the Naga underground movement gained strength.

The result of the awakening of the Nagas who had fought in France in the First World War, was an association called the Naga club formed in 1918 with the joint efforts of the headmen, and Government officials. This club had Nagas drawn from a number of Naga tribes. In 1929, the Naga club submitted a representation to the Simon Commission, wherein the Nagas stated that they wished to be left out from the proposed reformed scheme of India. They preferred to be under the direct administration of the British. The Government however did not agree and merely clubbed the Naga areas as Excluded Areas.

At this stage a development occurred that probably set the future leaders of the Naga underground, thinking that there should be a separate homeland for the Naga people of India and Myanmar. In 1941 Sir Robert Reid, the former Deputy Commissioner of the Naga Hills district, and the Governor of Assam, realising the ethnic and cultural differences of the Northeastern and Burma tribes, from the mainland Indians and Burmese, recommended a scheme to carve out a Trust Territory, called Crown Colony, comprising the Naga Hills, Northeast Frontier Areas and the Hill areas in upper Burma. He wanted a Northeast Province vaguely embracing all the Hill Ranges from the Lushai Hills right round to the Balipara Frontier tracts in the North, embracing on the way the Chittagong Hill Tracts, the Chins of Burma and perhaps the Shan states too, which would be directly administered by Whitehall. The Nagas themselves opposed it, for they were keen that the British had to go.

Then came the Second World War and the Japanese invasion of Burma followed by their attempt to enter India through Manipur and the Naga Hills. The Nagas were fully involved in the extensive fighting that erupted in Ukhrul and in the Naga Hills. While the majority supported the British, a small group joined the I.N.A. After the war the Deputy Commissioner of Naga Hills, launched an organisation called the Naga Hills District Council to repair the damages of war. However in April 1946, in its Wokha session, it was rechristened as the Naga National Council (N.N.C.) In June 1946, the N.N.C. submitted a four-point memorandum to the British Cabinet Mission who came to prepare the ground for granting independence to India. The four points were:

1. The Naga National Council stands for solidarity of Naga tribes, including those in the unadministered areas.

2. The Council strongly protests against the grouping of Assam with Bengal.

3. The Naga Hills should be constitutionally included in autonomous Assam, with local autonomy and due safeguard for the interest of the Nagas.

The reply of Jawaharlal Nehru, the then Congress President, in August 1946, though sympathetic, clearly rejected any independent status for the Nagas. In February 1947, the N.N.C sent a memorandum to Lord Mountbatten, the then Viceroy requesting setting up an interim government for the Nagas, for a period of 10 years, after which they would choose a form of government as they wished. In May 1947, a meeting with the Advisory committee of aboriginal tribes ended in a deadlock. Nehru then sent Sir Akbar Hydari, the Governor of Assam to discuss the issue with the Naga leaders. A nine-point agreement was signed. The last point, not very happily worded, was interpreted differently by the N.N.C. and the Government of India. A.Z. Phizo, who was just emerging as a new leader, began to spread the word that the Government of India was going back on its word. At this stage the N.N.C. had two groups, the moderates and the die hards, led by Phizo. In July 1947, Phizo led a six-member group of the die hards to Delhi. Phizo and his group returned empty handed, and promptly on August 14, 1947 the N.N.C. declared Naga National Independence, signed by nine members. In Kohima and Mokokchung, school students took part in the Naga National Independence ceremony. On the next day, the celebration of India's independence day was boycotted. These two incidents showed clearly that Phizo and his die-hard group had done their groundwork well. Phizo's group gradually gained control of the N.N.C. In 1948, the draft constitution of India was published. There was no mention of the nine-point agreement. In December, Phizo, advocated for a sovereign Naga state. Some of the moderate members tried once more for the implementation of the nine-point agreement, and another delegation was sent to Delhi. Beyond assurances that the constitution had all the safeguards required, it became clear that the Government of India had no intention to implement the nine-point agreement. The moderates felt let down and realised that the Indian Government was perfidious. In April 1950, the N.N.C. decided to establish a separate state of Nagaland. In December 1950, Phizo was elected as the President of the N.N.C. He was in full control of the N.N.C. and was recognised as the leader of the Naga national movement.

The moderates were virtually silenced. The N.N.C had a grand conference of representatives of several tribes at Kohima in May 1950, in which a resolution was passed to have a plebiscite for independence. This was conducted in May 1951. The genuineness of this plebiscite was questionable, but it was this plebiscite that directly led to a boycott of the first general election in 1952. Not a single vote was cast. Two years later, Phizo raised an armed body in Tuensang, called the Naga Home Guard, which developed into the Naga underground army. They were armed with Second World War weapons recovered from dumps left behind by the British.[8] There were some members of the N.N.C. who were still moderate and did not believe in violence. Among these were T. Sakhrie, J.B. Jasokie, T.N. Angami, and Dr. Imkongliba Ao, who resigned. In 1955 the Indian Army was deployed and the Assam Disturbed Areas Act was enacted and promulgated in the Naga Hills District.

In the same year, the N.N.C. set up the Federal Government of Nagaland (F.G.N.) and drew up a constitution envisaging a parliament of 100 Tatars (members of parliament) and a Kedhage (President), with a cabinet of 15 Kilonsers (Ministers). In addition, Deputy Commissioners and other officials were appointed. A whole parallel administration, both civil and military had come up. By 1956, the strength of the Naga Army had shot up to 15,000. In January 1956, Sakhrie was shot dead for cooperating with the Indian Government. Phizo escaped to East Pakistan, and after tying up with the Pakistan army reached London. Despite the quick expansion of the F.G.N. and the Naga Army, there was a sizeable moderate group still operating though several of their stalwarts were killed by the

Underground. The moderates organised an all tribes Naga people's convention in Kohima in August 1957, attended by 1,765 delegates and 2,000 visitors, representing every tribe. The resolution adopted was for a negotiated settlement of the Naga issue, and for setting up the Tuensang division of N.E.F.A. and the Naga Hills district of Assam under the External Affairs Ministry. The government as a consequence did set up a Naga Hills Tuensang area under the External Affairs Ministry. On the Underground side, the Manipur Naga Council formed in 1956, merged with the N.N.C. The years 1958 and 1959 saw intense activity by the moderate Naga People's Convention (N.P.C.). They held conventions in both these years at Ungma and Mokokchung, despite threats by the underground, in which they drafted a 16-point resolution for the constitution of a separate state called Nagaland. The Government of India accepted this resolution with little modification and the new state of Nagaland was inaugurated in December 1963. The underground opposed it vehemently, and the N.N.C. refused to recognise the new state.

An undeclared war had begun in the Naga Hills in 1955. Soon the fighting had become too serious for the Assam Rifles. The 8th Mountain Division of the Indian Army was inducted, reinforced by Assam Rifles and several armed police battalions. With so many armed forces deployed, excesses were bound to take place, and they did. The Naga insurgents by now, had a regular army, armed with rifles sten guns and some machine guns, organised in four commands. It is easy to write now with the benefit of hindsight, but the Government of India and the Indian Army made several strategic mistakes. After the Second World

War, a series of insurgencies broke out in South East Asia, in Malaya, the Philippines, and North Vietnam, all as a sequel to the revolution that brought the Communists to power in China. The 1950s were the decade of insurgencies and the best literature on counter-insurgency is of this period. Robert Thompson's classic, and the bible of all counter-insurgency dates from this period. The first lesson for any counter-insurgency is to find the cause, analyse it and take drastic steps to effect remedial measures. In the case of the Naga insurgency, there were no causes of malgovernance, of corruption and discrimination, by the Indian Government, though there was some poor handling by the Assam State Government, of neglect of the hill districts. This, however, was not the reason for the Nagas to take up arms against the Indian Government. Their point was that they did not want to be with India. One could not do anything to remedy this situation.

The second lesson is to ensure that in operations the people are not alienated. In a situation where there has been economic discrimination and corrupt governance, ensuring that there is good clean governance, can wean the people away from the insurgents. In the case of the Nagas, one had to be doubly careful, not to alienate the people, and to show them that being with the Government of India would not in any way disturb their culture, or their traditions and way of life. Unfortunately the Armed Forces, and the Paramilitary Forces operating, did commit excesses, which alienated the people. One of the biggest mistakes made was the regrouping of villages, taken from the example of Malaya. What the planners did not understand was that in Malaya, the villages regrouped were of Chinese settlers who were working as rubber tappers in the British rubber plantations. They were all Chinese immigrants and had no attachment to the places where they had built temporary shacks. In Nagaland, the Naga villages were hundreds of years old, each with its own rice paddies, either terraced or jhum fields, its forests, its sacred groves. Uprooting the inhabitants from such villages was akin to sacrilege, and it is no wonder that the Nagas hated the armed forces that perpetrated this. This alone was a totally insensitive and thoughtless act. Added to this were dozens of instances of torture and third degree. Robert Thompson has repeatedly emphasised that in a counter-insurgency the Forces deployed should be scrupulously legal. Here it is the Government of India that is to be faulted. They never tried to involve the judiciary in the counter insurgency grid. We have repeated this mistake again and again, in the counter-insurgency operations in Mizoram, Assam, Punjab, Kashmir, Tripura, and Manipur.

The third major mistake they made was the policy of the Central Government, or rather the political party who ruled from Delhi then, of thoroughly corrupting the local politicians and bureaucrats. After splitting the N.N.C. and the Underground Naga leadership, and granting statehood, development money was poured into the state, without any accountability. A notorious gang of contractors sprung up all based in Delhi, all followers of the party in power. It soon attained the dubious distinction of being called the 'Delhi Durbar.' All the major contracts of the state, all contracts for supply of stores went to this unholy gang, who brought 95 per cent of all development money sanctioned to the state back to Delhi, by the simple expedient of carrying out projects on paper, supplying stores on paper. This infamous band of contractors built three and four-star hotels, farmhouses and palaces in and around Delhi with this ill-gotten loot. The effect on the state was devastating, and the insurgency which began without any grounds of discrimination or poor governance, got all the reasons for an insurgency, and the main reasons for its continuing so long is because of this one facet. I had worked as Superintendent of Police of the C.B.I. in Shillong and investigated several cases involving, the Delhi Durbar. All the big cases involving lakhs and crores of rupees were closed on political intervention from Delhi, because they involved hangers on of the party in power.

The incidents of violence continued unabated, but the underground was divided, with the Tuensang and Sema group leaving them. The Nagas had boycotted the 1952 and 1957 elections, but now with the state formed, elections had to be held. Two parties were formed, the Democratic Party and the Nagaland National Organisation (N.N.O.) The first wanted the independence of Nagaland, while the second spoke of the peace and economic progress of the state. Phizo had promised to come, but dropped out at the last moment. The N.N.O. won 28 seats and the Democratic Front 12.

The incidents of violence did not abate. By now a link had been established with the I.S.I. of Pakistan, and the F.G.N. had a base in Dacca. Self-styled General Kaito Sema had led a group of hostiles through Paren subdivision, North Cachar Hills, Jaintia Hills into East Pakistan and established training camps there. The first supplies of arms from the Pakistan Army were also received—rifles, light machine guns and mortars. Some of the hostiles were also trained in explosives. S.S. General Kaito Sema brought the group of hostiles trained in East Pakistan, and a small unit was located on Agotito hill overlooking the stretch of Dodar Ali, the old road built by the Ahom kings. Using this as a base, small parties would be sent to lay explosives on the rail track of the N.E.Frontier Railway. The Assam Mail the only mail train from Delhi to Dibrugarh was derailed several times between 1964 and 1967. Worse, at least twice explosives placed in a trunk and left behind in a crowded carriage, exploded killing and maiming innocent passengers. In Nagaland and Manipur, ambushes by hostiles on Security Force convoys were a regular feature. The security forces retaliated and very frequently the civilian population suffered from excesses committed. The F.G.N. had also sent several groups to China, who were trained by the Chinese army and who brought back assorted arms, rifles, light machine guns and mortars. Deeply disturbed at the escalating violence the Third Baptist Convention at Wokha requested the Central Government through the State Government to set up a Peace Mission. The Government of India approved the request and a Peace Mission was constituted. With the help of the Baptist Church leaders the Peace Mission met the Underground leaders. After several discussions and arguments, a cease-fire agreement was signed in September 1964, and peace talks began between the two delegations. Many rounds of talks were held in Nagaland but the results were fruitless, and the talks were adjourned to the political level at Delhi. Several rounds of talks at Delhi did not yield any results either and after a deadlock, the F.G.N. delegation returned empty-handed.

The Achilles' heel of the Nagas was inter-tribal rivalry, and the Intelligence Bureau did its best to take advantage of this. Soon after the Naga delegation returned, differences between Kaito Sema and the Angami group sharpened, and Mowu Angami replaced Kaito Sema as the chief of the Naga Federal army. On the civil side, Mehiasiu Angami replaced Scatu Swu Sema as the President of the F.G.N. Both Mowu Angami and Mehiasiu were Angamis from Khonoma, the village of Phizo. Two other appointments sealed the issue. Two Thankhul Nagas from Manipur were appointed, Z. Ramyo as Home Minister and Thuingaleng Muivah as General Secretary of the N.N.C. As the Semas were reacting to this, Kaito Sema was assassinated in Kohima. The Semas retaliated by kidnapping both Mehiasiu Angami and Z. Ramyo, and then formed a new group, the Revolutionary Government of Nagaland (R.G.N.) Shortly thereafter, the first group of Naga hostiles who had gone to China returned with arms led by Thinuselie and Th. Muivah. The Indian Army intercepted them and several skirmishes ensued. Twenty-five hostiles were captured and 7.62 rifles, mortars seized from them, besides incriminating documents, which showed that, the Chinese government was very much involved in training and equipping them. The R.G.N. was meanwhile actively helping the Indian Army, and were instrumental in the capture of Mowu Angami. The split in the F.G.N. widened and finally the R.G.N. surrendered to the Government of India in August 1973. A number of their soldiers were taken into the Border Security Force.

With the failure of the talks between the Government of India and the F.G.N. the cease-fire was abrogated and the situation again escalated. There was an attempt to assassinate the Chief Minister Hokishe Sema. His convoy was ambushed and several of his escorts were killed. The ambush was arranged probably because the Naga affairs were transferred from the External affairs to the Home Ministry.[9] At this point Nagaland Church leaders and Sarvodaya workers formed the Nagaland Peace Council in mid-1974. This council worked quietly and without publicity. They found that several of the underground leaders had mellowed. After months of extensive ground work, the Peace Council brought the group of underground leaders who had changed their stand to the Chedema peace camp, and finally arranged for talks between the Government of India and a group of six underground leaders led by Kevi Yallya, Phizo's brother at the Raj Bhavan Shillong.[10] A peace accord was signed on November 11, 1975. There were three paras:

1. The underground of their own volition would accept without condition the Constitution of India.

2. The arms now underground would be brought out and deposited.

3. The leaders of the underground would formulate other issues for discussion and final settlement.

The Unlawful Activities Act which was enforced after the ambush of Hokishe Sema, the Chief Minister was withdrawn. Later the F.G.N. met at Dihoma and the President Zashi Huire, Home Minister, Biseto Medom and the Chief of the Army Vijalie Mehta endorsed the agreement.[11] Probably there were two reasons why the leadership of the Underground accepted the accord. The leadership had been divided since 1973, and the N.N.O. was hampering the activities of the underground. The Chinese support was not substantial.[12] At the time of the run up to the Shillong Accord, Isaac Swu and Thuingaleng Muivah were on their way back from China. They denounced the accord. They appealed to Phizo to denounce the Accord. Strangely, Phizo did not respond publicly, but privately said that the signatories were puppets. After trying for five years to restore the image of the N.N.C., Isaac Swu and Muivah who were camping with S.S. Kaphlang, the Hemi Naga from Myanmar abandoned the N.N.O. and formed the National Socialist Council of Nagaland (N.S.C.N.) along with S.S. Kaphlang on January 31, 1980. They replaced the F.G.N. with the Government of People's Republic of Nagaland (G.P.R.N.)

With the creation of the N.S.C.N., the insurgency in Nagaland took a completely new turn. The F.G.N. and the Naga Army had gone to East Pakistan and China and obtained arms and were trained there, but they did not link up with any other insurgent group operating in the North East. From its inception, the N.S.C.N. was linked up with the Peoples Liberation Army (P.L.A.) of Manipur, and the United Liberation Front of Assam (U.L.F.A.) of Assam. Besides these two groups, the N.S.C.N. has adopted more than a dozen insurgent groups of the Northeast, helped them to procure arms, trained them, and extorted money along with them. The N.S.C.N. thus extended their financial net well beyond Nagaland, and since their participation with other groups was generally in a ratio of 8:2, their share of the money extorted by these groups was generally in the same proportion. It was the N.S.C.N. who patronised the U.L.F.A. and took them to Kaphlang's area and arranged for their training there. Later they helped the National Democratic Front of Boroland (N.D.F.B.), the Boro militant group. The Nagas and the Kuki-Chin-Mizo group were traditional enemies. The old Naga underground and the

Mizo National Front (M.N.F.) lived in separate houses in Dacca, and never had any link in the Northeast. After the Mizo settlement in 1989, when the Hmars demand for a district council was not conceded by the Mizo Government, and they formed the Hmar People's Convention (H.P.C.) it was the N.S.C.N. (I.M.) who adopted them and gave them weapons and trained them. They set up camps in the North Cachar Hills, and committed several bank robberies in the interior of Cachar district, and carried out many ambushes on security forces along with the H.P.C. cadres. In Meghalaya, when the Hynniewtrep National Liberation Council (H.N.L.C.) and the Achik National Volunteer Council (A.N.V.C.) started minor insurgencies against the Government, it was the N.S.C.N. (I.M.) who befriended them and helped them with arms and trained them. Back in the North Cachar Hills, the Dimasa Cachari formed a guerilla group called the Dima Halem Daoga (D.H.D.), because of the rampant corruption of the District Council. It was the N.S.C.N. who held their hand, gave them arms and trained them. The United Peoples Democratic Solidarity (U.P.D.S.) an insurgent group of the Karbis of Assam was raised in 1999 to fight for a separate state .The N.S.C.N. (I.M.) armed and trained this group. A major share of the extortion by all these groups went to the N.S.C.N. In Tripura both the National Liberation Front of Tripura (N.L.F.T) and the All Tripura Tiger Force (A.T.T.F.) were again armed and trained by the N.S.C.N. (I.M.). In Manipur the N.S.C.N. (I.M.) has strong links with the K.Y.K.L. (O), a Meithei insurgent group, which runs a big extortion net in the Imphal valley. They have also allied with the Zomi Reunification Army (Z.R.A.), the United Kuki Liberation Front (U.K.L.F.) and the Kuki Revolutionary Army (K.R.A.) all without any ideology and purely involved in extortion. Here the share of money extorted for the N.S.C.N. is a clear 80 per cent. It is no wonder then that the N.S.C.N. (I.M.) is a fabulously rich organisation and can afford to maintain offices in Bangkok, Manila and the Netherlands. The N.S.C.N. (I.M.) is no more an ideological guerrilla group. It has made a business enterprise out of insurgencies and made an export oriented industry out of it. I wonder if the old guard of the Naga Underground has realised this.

The N.S.C.N. set up its H.Q.s in Hemi Naga country in northern Burma. Bertil Lintner has vividly described his visit to this H.Q.s, marching from Longwa village, on the trijunction of Nagaland, Khonsa, and Myanmar for several days traversing several ranges.[13] Several U.L.F.A. cadres whom I had interrogated also described this route. One fact that finds mention by Bertil Lintner and many U.L.F.A. cadres was that in the H.Q.s of the N.S.C.N., the Thangkhul and the Konyak did not seem to get on well, and they had established separate camps. The old devil of tribal rivalry was at work again, and ultimately it led to the break up of the N.S.C.N. into two factions. The main feature of the N.S.C.N. setting up its camp in Hemi Naga country was the connection established with the Kachin Independent Organisation (K.I.O.) and its army wing the K.I.A. The second feature was the link established with the P.L.A. of Manipur, who had come to the K.I.O. for training and arms. After the disastrous election in Assam in 1984, the militant students of the All Assam Students Union (A.A.S.U.) had formed the U.L.F.A., and they requested the N.S.C.N. for arms and training. The N.S.C.N. brought the U.L.F.A. cadres first to Kaphlangs H.Q.s and then to the K.I.O. area. Cadres of the N.S.C.N., U.L.F.A. and the P.L.A., after receiving tough training returned to Nagaland, Manipur and Assam and started operating in their respective areas. Extensive extortion from the business community in all the three states started, for the Kachins while imparting excellent training also charged high rates particularly for the weapons. Meanwhile, inter tribal feelings in the N.S.C.N. camp were getting exacerbated, and in 1988 boiled over in a violent clash in which several top leaders of Th.Muivah and Isaac Swu were killed. Muivah and Swu retreated to Nagaland and Manipur and the N.S.C.N. split into two factions, N.S.C.N. (I.M.) and N.S.C.N. (K) Meanwhile Indian intelligence had won over Bronsen, the President of the K.I.O. and he withdrew support to the N.S.C.N., P.L.A., and the U.L.F.A. Sensing this development, the P.L.A. had already arranged safe houses in Srimangal, Adams Bazaar and Chotto Dhamai in Sylhet district of Bangladesh, among the Meithei settlers there. The U.L.F.A. had also sent parties to Bangladesh to see if they could get sanctuary there. All three groups had independently visited China. Though they could buy some weapons, they did not get substantial support. The move to Bangladesh was a kind of last-ditch attempt to survive. None of the three groups had any love for Bangladesh who kept exporting their population to all the states of the Northeast. Little did they know that the link developing with Bangladesh would change the situation drastically in their favour and they were on the threshold of an arms bonanza.

The Assamese were the first to strike gold. They were able to get in touch with a group that took them to the Pakistan embassy. Very soon they were talking to the I.S.I. man in Dacca, who immediately realised that here was a heaven sent opportunity to subvert India in a sensitive but wholly unexpected quarter. With the help of the Bangladesh Directorate General Forces Intelligence (D.G.F.I.) ten of the U.L.F.A. cadres were given Bangladeshi names and passports and found themselves bound for Karachi. They were taken to Peshawar and put in a camp of the Afghan Mujahideen of Gulbuddin Hekmatyar. This was in 1991.Three such groups were trained on medium weapons, rocket launchers and mortars. Back in Bangladesh in a safe house arranged by the D.G.F.I. the I.S.I. gave a task to the U.L.F.A. to send its cadres back to Assam and blow up the refinery at Narangi. The young Assamese boys who were given this task objected and said they were not willing to damage their own assets. There was a fight with Paresh Barua, their self-styled chief, and the ten boys who had been given this task, slipped out of the safe house and deserting Paresh Barua returned to Assam. As Inspector General Operations in Assam some of our sources informed me of this transaction and asked me if I would meet these boys. Very soon we were debriefing them and the whole story was pieced together. The N.S.C.N. (I.M.) leaders soon joined the U.L.F.A. in Bangladesh, and Th. Muivah and Paresh Baruah had Bangladeshi names and passports given to them. Meetings with the I.S.I. followed, and they were told that after the breakup of the Khmer Rogue, in Cambodia, a lot of Russian small arms were available with arms dealers in Thailand. These could be purchased and brought in local trawlers that sailed along the Myanmar coast. One of the U.L.F.A. cadres who had been arrested and agreed to work with us, told us of a meeting held in Sayeman Hotel in Cox's Bazaar where Th.Muivah, Paresh Barua along with I.S.I. and D.G.F.I. officers, finalised this deal.

Some time towards the latter half of 1991, the D.I.G. Operations Mizoram informed Assam Police H.Q.s, that a party of Nagas had marched south along the eastern border of Mizoram, in Myanmar and turning west at the southernmost point of Mizoram, Parva, had entered Bangladesh. The party had generally marched through Myanmar, but sometimes entered Mizoram border villages to buy rations. No force was deployed along the eastern border of Mizoram, and no spare troops were available. Hence no interception was attempted. The reason for the movement was not known at that point of time. Sometime later, 10 Naga boys surrendered to the B.S.F. post at Parva. They were brought to Massimpur and interrogated, and then the real story came to light. The ten Naga boys, who were all N.S.C.N. (I.M.) cadres revealed that a party of 250 cadres of the group had set out from Paren subdivision of Nagaland, and marching through Tamenglong, Churachandpur crossed south into Myanmar, and then followed the Tiddim road, skirted the eastern border of Mizoram, and finally crossed into Bangladesh south and east of Parva, and reached Bandarban. After a long wait the ten boys got fed up with the harsh conditions of the march and the living conditions and decided to return to Nagaland. They ran away from the camp, but were chased by their colleagues, and hence decided to surrender to the B.S.F. at Parva. They further added that they were sent to collect a consignment of arms, which was to be landed at Cox's Bazaar. It was later on corroborated that these arms had been purchased from arms dealers in Thailand with the help of the I.S.I. and brought to Cox's Bazaar by a coastal vessel. The arms were collected by the 240 N.S.C.N. (I.M.) party and taken back to Nagaland along the route they had followed when coming down.

Incidentally, the D.I.G. Operations Mizoram tracked their return movement, but since there were no troops they could not be intercepted. The N.S.C.N. (I.M.) had got its first consignment of arms from Thailand with the help of the I.S.I. and the D.G.F.I. Subsequently at least three more consignments of arms were brought. The later consignments were for the N.S.C.N. (I.M.), U.L.F.A., P.L.A. and the N.D.F.B. The weapons brought were A.K.rifles, R.P.D.7.62 L.M.G.s, R.P.G.-7 rocket launchers and Chinese grenades. During this period, the D.G.F.I helped the N.S.C.N. (I.M.), U.L.F.A. and the N.D.F.B. to set up camps for training their cadres in the Chittagong Hill Tracts. All these three organisations set up safe houses in Dacca, Cox's Bazaar, and other towns along their routes of ingress into Bangladesh. Evidence of the weapons received by the three insurgent groups was clearly manifested by enhanced operations by all three groups in Assam, Nagaland and Manipur.

It was during this period that the N.S.C.N. (I.M.) began to expand its operations. In Meghalaya, an underground group called the Hynniewtrep Achik Liberation Council (H.A.L.C.) had come up. The N.S.C.N. (I.M.) had safe houses in Shillong, to facilitate movement of their cadres to Bangladesh, through Naljuri and Dawki, and further west through Nongstoin and Garo Hills. The H.A.L.C. soon split up into Khasi and Garo groups called Hynniewtrep National Liberation Council (H.N.L.C.) and the Achik National Volunteer Council (A.N.V.C.). Both the groups contacted the N.S.C.N. (I.M.) for help, which was immediately given. Both groups were helped to set up training camps in Diengling for the H.N.L.C. and in the thick jungles of east and west Garo Hills for the A.N.V.C. The N.S.C.N.'s main interest was in the money to be garnered from this link. Shillong was a rich area for extortion. There were extensive collections from the rich Marwari traders. A series of kidnappings by the two outfits also yielded rich dividends. The politicians acted as go betweens in the release of kidnapped officials and business heads and took a share, but the major share went to the N.S.C.N. (I.M.)

We have already seen the link between the N.S.C.N. (I.M.) and the H.P.C. in the North Cachar Hills. The Hmar People's Convention took to arms because they felt that the Mizos were discriminating against them in development in Mizoram. The Hmars were a part of the larger Kuki-Chin-Mizo group. They did create problems in Mizoram, but then had no reason to extend their operations to the North Cachar Hills of Assam. There was a considerable population of Hmars in the N.C. Hills, and a few villages in Cachar district, including Hmarkholian—one of the largest villages in Cachar. There was no love lost between the Nagas and the Mizos. The Naga insurgency started in 1955, while the Mizo insurgency started in 1966. Though both parties went to East Pakistan for help, there was never any axis between them. When the Hmars decided to take up arms against the Mizos, the N.S.C.N. (I.M.) extended a hand. The real reason for this was that the N.S.C.N (I.M.) wanted to get a foothold in the N.C.Hills, where there was a small Zemi Naga population. N.S.C.N. cadres with a few H.P.C. cadres led the small guerilla bands formed, that operated in the N.C. Hills and in Cachar. The N.S.C.N. (I.M.) cadres never operated in Mizoram. The other reason was the scope for extortion. There were a number of good tea gardens in the lower slopes of the N.C. Hills and in the foothills in Cachar. The N.S.C.N.

(I.M.) cadres led the H.P.C in kidnapping tea garden managers, and issuing ransom notes. They even tried to rob some small banks in Cachar district. The countryside of the N.C. Hills was poor, but the N.S.C.N. (I.M.) did not hesitate to extort money from small traders in the towns. Much later when the Dimasas started their own insurgent group, the Dima Halem Daoga, in N.C. Hills, the N.S.C.N. (I.M.) again backed them, training them and equipping them with arms, and of course extorting money from corrupt government officials, and kidnapping for ransom. The major share of the extorted money went to the N.S.C.N. (I.M.) It is only when the demand for inclusion of N.C. Hills in greater Nagaland came up that the Dimasas realised that they had been taken for a ride. There are a few Zemi Naga villages in N.C.Hills. Population wise the Zemi Naga are the smallest; the Kukis and the Hmars are much greater in number. The Dimasa are the major community. There is no case for the whole or even a part of N.C. Hills being included in Greater Nagaland. When the U.P.D.S. of Karbi Anglong asked for help, the N.S.C.N. (I.M.) was only too glad to help. This suited their objectives since there was a small minority of Rengmas and Zemis in Karbi Anglong. Here again the ratio of pay offs to the N.S.C.N. (I.M.) from the moneys extorted from the non-Karbis and traders was 8:2. Later, when the N.S.C.N. (I.M.) laid claim to the Karbi Anglong district for Greater Nagaland, the U.P.D.S. realised that they had been taken for a ride and cut off relations.

It is in Manipur that the N.S.C.N. (I.M.) has played its biggest games. The Meithei from the valley and the Naga from the hills have not been well disposed to each other ever since the Naga insurgency started in 1955. The Meitheis uneasily watched as the Nagas got a state in 1963, while they still remained a Union Territory. Later as the N.S.C.N. (I.M.) gained strength the Meitheis who had ruled over Manipur and a major part of Nagaland for hundreds of years, began to feel threatened. The Manipur valley and particularly Imphal was a rich ground for extortion. The pickings from Ukhrul, Senapati and Tamenglong were meagre. So, when Namoijam Oken Singh left the United National Liberation Front (U.N.L.F.) and later formed the Kanglei Yawol Kanna Lup (K.Y.K.L.), the N.S.C.N. (I.M.) sent a feeler that they could supply arms and also train their cadres. Oken accepted the offer, thereby giving a foothold to the N.S.C.N. (I.M.) in Imphal.

The Nagas and the Kukis were ancient foes. The Meithei kings effectively used the Kuki as a buffer against the Nagas. The British later picked a leaf from the Meitheis and continued to use the Kuki as a buffer. When the N.S.C.N. (I.M.), was getting strong, Indian intelligence fell back on the same idea and propped up the Kukis as the Kuki National Organisation. (K.N.O.), and the (K.N.A.) to fight the Nagas. The ploy turned out to be a disaster as it unleashed an ethnic war, and a number of Kuki villages which were in Naga areas in Ukhrul, and Tamenglong were burnt and the Kukis became the victims of ethnic cleansing. Leadership squabbles split the K.N.O. into several groups—K.N.F (M.C.), K.N.F. (Presidential). During the election of 1998, two more groups were spawned due to tickets being denied to two Kuki leaders who promptly formed two insurgent groups, the United Kuki Liberation Front (U.K.L.F.) and the Kuki Revolutionary Army (K.R.A.). Both these organisations needed weapons and training, and they had no choice but to go to the ancient enemy the N.S.C.N. (I.M.). Both these groups operated in small bands, generally in a ratio of 8:2. The money collected in extensive extortion operations was also divided in the same ratio, 8 for the N.S.C.N. and 2 for the U.K.L.F. or K.R.A.

The third penetration of the Kuki-Chin-Mizo group was of the Zomi Reunification Army, which was formed in 1993 with the objective of unifying the Chins living in Myanmar and India. The K.N.A. was set up to take on the N.S.C.N. (I.M.). The bait offered was control of the rich spoils of smuggling in Moreh, the border town of Manipur in Chandel district. The reaction of the N.S.C.N. (I.M.) was unexpectedly fierce. The K.N.A. was battered, and the fight was taken to the villages. There were a number of Kuki villages in Ukhrul and Tamenglong, and these were attacked, burnt and the hapless Kukis rendered homeless. The K.N.A. approached their brethren in Churachandpur for help. While some of the related tribes agreed to help, the Paites, a sister tribe of the Zomi, refused, saying that the Kukis had no business to take on the N.S.C.N. (I.M.). Infuriated, the K.N.A. attacked the Paites. The internecine fight went badly for the Paites. They generally lived on the southern borders of Churachandpur with Myanmar. South of the border was N.S.C.N. (I.M.) country. Driven to the wall the Paites who had formed the Z.R.O. had no choice but to ask the N.S.C.N. (I.M.) for help. The Z.R.O., which till than had only a few arms, now got a substantial supply of arms and training from the N.S.C.N. (I.M.). The Paites were the best businessmen of all the tribes of the Chin-Mizo-Kuki group, and they were good smugglers. The objective of the N.S.C.N. (I.M.) was well achieved. They had penetrated the Kuki-Chin-Mizo group, and they got a share of the smuggling and trade revenues of the Paites.

By the mid-1990s, the N.S.C.N. (I.M.) had a well-oiled extortion net in place in Nagaland, Manipur, including the non-Naga areas, in the N.C. Hills, and in Meghalaya. In Nagaland and in Ukhrul, Senapati, Tamenglong and part of Chandel district, standard collection of house tax and ration contribution of paddy was routinely being collected. Besides, all trucks and buses going from Dimapur to parts of Nagaland and to Manipur were taxed. All development projects were also monitored and government officials and contractors had to pay a share. They also had an annual supply of arms coming in from Thailand brought in coastal vessels to Cox's Bazaar, and brought overland via Bandarban, Parva, along the eastern border of Mizoram, north on the Tiddim road, through Churachandpur, Tamenglong to Paren subdivision of Nagaland. The considerable extortion revenues coming in from several sources helped them to open offices in Bangkok, Manila and Holland. They also had several camps in the C.H.T. and safe houses in Dacca, Chittagong. Then they had a big setback. The Indian Army along with the intelligence agencies had carefully been monitoring the collection of arms from Thailand, it's being shipped to Cox's Bazaar and carried overland to Nagaland, by the N.S.C.N. (I.M). In the winter of 1995, when probably the fourth or fifth consignment was being carried they ambushed the foot convoy west of Parva in a well-planned operation that caught the N.S.C.N. (I.M.), U.L.F.A., and the N.D.F.B., who comprised the party by surprise. Several cadres of all three parties were killed, some were captured and a sizeable number of arms were seized. Altogether 58 cadres of the three groups were killed, and 40 captured. The operation was aptly named Golden Bird.

Meanwhile the Government of India at the political level was trying to get the N.S.C.N. (I.M.) leaders to come to the negotiating table. Th. Muivah and Isaac Swu laid down three conditions. The negotiations should focus on security, the talks must be in a third country and there should be a third party mediator. The government agreed to the first two conditions, but not the third. After several discussions, the N.S.C.N. (I.M.) agreed. Talks commenced and they agreed to a cease-fire from August 1, 1997. A cease-fire monitoring group was set up, and ground rules framed. There was to be no killing kidnapping or extortion by the N.S.C.N. (I.M.) and no active military operations against N.S.C.N. (I.M.) by the security forces. N.S.C.N. (I.M.) camps in notified places could be maintained, but the group would not patrol with arms. They could move from camp to camp concealing their arms. The cease-fire was for Nagaland. Unofficially it was allowed in the Naga districts of Manipur. This concession was a cardinal mistake, and was to cost the government later.

From day one, the cease-fire monitoring group was a farce. The operations of the security forces discontinued, as also of the N.S.C.N. (I.M.). Extortion by them, however, continued unabated, though there were no killings for failure to pay, at least by the N.S.C.N. (I.M.). It is here that the N.S.C.N. (I.M.) played a clever trick on the Government of India. In Manipur they had alliances with the K.Y.K.L., U.K.L.F., K.R.A, and Z.R.O. In all their operations, N.S.C.N. (I.M.) cadres operated along with them. When accosted by the cease-fire monitoring group, the innocent reply was that it was an operation of the K.Y.K.L, or U.K.L.F. The incident which took place in Chandel in November 2000 is a clear example of the perfidy of the N.S.C.N. (I.M.) On Friday November 24, 2000, a group of 30 N.S.C.N. (I.M.) and U.K.L.F. cadres, kidnapped the Deputy Commissioner Chandel, disarmed and then locked up his Manipur Rifles escort, and forced him to call five of his Block Development Officers and made them sign five cheques totaling Rs. 44.8 lakhs, District Rural Development grants coming directly from the Central Government. Since by that time the bank was closed, the brigands kept the D.C., the B.D.O.s and the D.C.s escort confined through Saturday and Sunday, and on Monday cashed the cheques and releasing the D.C., B.D.O.s and the escort, disappeared with Rs. 44.8 lakhs development grant. Chandel was the most backward and the poorest district in Manipur. When the Central Government was informed, the Cease Fire Monitoring Group was asked to ensure the money was returned. When the N.S.C.N. (I.M.) H.Q. took it up with their Chandel unit they refused to return the money and took cover behind the U.K.L.F., stating, that this was their operation.

In accordance with the Cease-Fire Agreement, the N.S.C.N. (I.M.) was not to procure any arms. A number of incidents and interrogation reports of N.S.C.N. (I.M.) cadres reveal that this insurgent group has steadily been procuring arms from abroad, right from 1997, when the Cease Fire Agreement was signed. The Assam Rifles had opened a platoon post in February 1999, near Amchurimukh in Mizoram because of the activities of the Bru National Liberation Front (B.N.L.F.). This was the first post on the Mizoram Bangladesh border after Tripura. On the night of March 3, 1999, the post received information that a large group of N.S.C.N. (I.M.) of about 110 cadres had crossed from Bangladesh between the last post of Tripura, Kanthlang and the first post of Mizoram, Amchurimukh. They were moving in five groups and two had already crossed, and entered the Lengai valley and were proceeding north. The Assam Rifles organised an immediate ambush, and managed to get the third group, who after marching through the night had stopped for a rest. The Assam Rifles managed to surprise them and killed 6 of the N.S.C.N.(I.M.) cadres, a collaborator and injured one who was taken and admitted in the civil hospital at Agartala. They recovered weapons from all the cadres killed and captured. A few days later, a party of N.S.C.N. (I.M.) from their H.Q.s at Dimapur met the Assam Rifles Brigadier and objected to the attack on their cadres during the cease-fire and asked for the return of the seized weapons. Here was a blatant case of bringing weapons from a neighbouring country, and when ambushed, accusing the security force of violating the cease-fire. What is most interesting is the last part of the episode. Instead of reinforcing the post, which lay bang on this route of bringing weapons from Bangladesh, the Assam Rifles withdrew this post. When I was visiting Tripura after this incident, the Chief Minister Manik Sarkar told me that the Assam Rifles had done an excellent job in ambushing the N.S.C.N. (I.M.) party while they were bringing arms, but inexplicably withdrew the post after the ambush. The mystery of the withdrawal of the post from Amchurimukh could never be solved.

Some time in the latter half of 2001, a group of five N.S.C.N. (I.M.) cadres surrendered with their weapons to the B.S.F. post at Parva. They were brought to Masimpur and interrogated, and told a most interesting tale. One of the five was a senior seargent of the Gallilee camp near Alikadam, Bandarban. He said that a large party of the N.S.C.N. (I.M.) had moved from Nagaland via the Tiddim road, Parva to Bandarban for collecting the arms consignment expected by the end of the year. Tired of the harsh living conditions, ten of the cadres had defected and run away with their arms, hoping to make it back to Nagaland. The main group had chased them and killed five of them, and so they surrendered to the B.S.F. post at Parva. Their interrogation revealed that the N.S.C.N. (I.M.) had the following camps: -

1. Jortan camp near Cox's Bazaar – strength 250
2. Vaital camp near Rangamati – strength 300
3. Galilee camp near Alikadam – strength 50
4. Mauni transit camp near Sylhet
5. H.Q.s of N.S.C.N. (I.M.) at Dacca. A four-storey building near New Market

The arms collected from Cox's Bazaar were supplied by China. Collection of weapons is generally done once a year. The route adopted was Cox's Bazaar, Alikadam, Kasalang Reserve Forest, Mizoram, Silchar, Jiribam, Tamenglong, and Paren. In July 2001, they delivered a consignment of 35 weapons – AK56-10, Sniper Rifle-8, M21-17 along with ammunition. The most interesting part is the next stage. The weapons were brought on foot upto Mizoram near Amchurimukh. From here it was sent by a Gypsy of the N.S.C.N. (I.M.) via Silchar, Jiribam, Tamenglong, Paren, and Dimapur. It has been subsequently verified that the N.S.C.N. (I.M.) has a safe house at Aizawl. Obviously the

Government of Mizoram has given the safe house. The movement of arms by road also could not take place without the patronage of the State Government.

On March 16, 2002, a party of N.S.C.N. (I.M.) cadres was moving from Chandel to Ukhrul. Near Pallel, a section of Manipur Rifles was manning a checkgate. When they saw the uniformed cadres moving in the vehicle, they challenged the vehicle and asked them to lay down their weapons. When challenged, the cadres opened fire. The Manipur Rifles guard immediately fired back. Eleven boys of the N.S.C.N. (I.M.) were killed and their weapons seized. There was a strong protest from the N.S.C.N. (I.M.) The State Government took the stand, that the underground cadres should not have moved with their weapons showing, and in any case when challenged, should have stopped. On March 25 the Deputy Commissioner of Chandel was kidnapped. The N.S.C.N. (I.M.) said it was in retaliation for the killing of their cadres. At this point the talks with the Government of India were stalled on this issue. The N.S.C.N. (I.M.) wanted the weapons returned in exchange for the D.C. I am told that a section in the government was willing to have the weapons returned. Fortunately the government stood firm and stated that if the D.C. were not released, the peace process would collapse. The D.C. was released unconditionally. This is a clear indication that, the top leadership of the N.S.C.N. (I.M.) is ready to climb down and they want the cease-fire to continue. The government has to be firm in dealing with them.

One other item of interest shows how the N.S.C.N.(I.M.) acts with duplicity. It was reported that a Chinese firm had encashed a crossed cheque of half a million dollars of the

N.S.C.N. (I.M.) for supply of A.K.47 rifles and machine guns in 2000. Anthony Shimray had organised this deal for the N.S.C.N. (I.M.).[14] The cease-fire was in force from 1997.

The case for sovereignty of the Nagas just does not exist. Not only does it not exist, but also it is based on an assumption that is fictitious, and has no basis in history. The first assumption that the Nagas existed as an independent entity from time immemorial is fictitious. The Nagas never even existed as a tribe. The Nagas' basic entity was a village. All the villages of a tribe were never organised, as an entity, never fought a war as a tribe. All that a village recognised was another village. The Ahoms who migrated to upper Assam in the 11th century established a kingdom that ruled over the whole of Assam. Well before that the Meitheis had established their kingdom in the 3rd century A.D. The whole of the present Nagaland was part of their kingdom. There is ample evidence of this from the first British civil and army officers. Right from the 1st century, Assam has seen several kingdoms, the Chutias, the Rajbongshis, and the Dimasa Cacharis. The last group had their capital at Dimapur. The second assumption that all the areas that have Naga villages should be in a Greater Nagaland is nothing unique in India. In 1956 the States Reorganisation tried to group all people of one particular language in a state. But could this be done to the last man? There are Tamil villages in Kerala, Malayali villages in Tamil Nadu, Telugu villages in Karnataka, Kannada villages in Andhra Pradesh. There are Jaintia villages in Bangladesh, Meithei settlements in Bangladesh, Naga villages in Myanmar. To allege that the British deliberately divided the Nagas between India and Burma is ridiculous. After the

Burmese army was driven back from upper Assam and Manipur, and obviously from the Naga areas in-between, the boundaries were roughly settled at the Treaty of Yandaboo. During all this period right down to the 19th century, the Naga way of life is best summed up by R.B. McCabe, "Grouped in small communities of from 100 to 3000 persons, the Nagas have remained isolated on their hill tops, only deigning to visit their immediate neighbours, when a longing for the possession of their heads became too strong to be resisted."

As a minority people in India, the Nagas, Mizos, Khasis and the different tribes in Arunachal, have all been treated with great circumspection by the Constitution of India. Their lands cannot be transferred to the non-tribals; their customary laws are in force in their respective states. One has only to look at our neighbour Bangladesh to see how they have treated the Chakmas of the C.H.T. Today their homeland has been overrun by plainsmen and they are now a minority in their own area. They are on the way of disappearing from the face of the earth, a human group facing extinction. I do not think there is a case, for any of the claims of the Nagas, neither for sovereignty, nor for a greater Nagaland. The Zemi Naga are a minority tribe in the N.C. Hills of Assam. Does it mean that the whole of N.C. Hills is to be given to a Greater Nagaland? The case of Karbi Anglong is the same. In Manipur it is a fact that successive State Governments have discriminated against all the hill districts. The answer is to extend the Sixth Schedule of the Constitution to the hill districts of Manipur, not dismember it.

The great mistake made by the Government of India

was that they did not study how the insurgencies in Malaya and the Philippines were tackled in the 1950s. In the entire hill states of the Northeast the first priority is to build fair weather roads so that all villages are connected to the towns. Unfortunately in Nagaland and Manipur, hundreds of kilometres of roads were built on paper. Roads are the first enemies of the insurgents. Denied of a hinterland he has no place to retreat. Today this is the first step to be taken by the Government of India. This task must be given to the Border Roads. The second task is to ensure clean administration for the people. The policy adopted by the party in power at the centre, in the 1950s and the 1960s, to flood the area with development funds and corrupt the politicians and the bureaucrats was a disaster. It only lined the coffers of the followers and lackeys of the party, the Delhi Durbar. The common man of Nagaland and Manipur is disgusted with paying house tax, ration tax, a percentage of his salary to bandits masquerading as insurgents. The task is not difficult, only the will to do it is required.

For Thuingaleng Muivah, the Thangkhul from Somdal and Isaac Swu, it has been a long journey. They were in China when a section of the N.N.O. defected and signed the Shillong agreement in 1975. It must have been particularly difficult for Isaac Swu, for it was the Semas who had defected in general and surrendered to the Government. With the formation of the N.S.C.N. with Kaphlang, the fight continued from Myanmar. The old devil of tribal rivalries caught up with them again, and the N.S.C.N. split. It was after this and with the movement to Bangladesh and the link with the Pakistan I.S.I., and the Bangladesh D.G.F.I., that the horizon of the group expanded beyond their expectations.

They could internationalise the problem to some extent, though ultimately, they could get no significant leverage from it. They have given in on two items before and during the dialogue with the Government of India. They gave up the demand for a mediator, and they agreed to release the Deputy Commissioner of Chandel without getting their arms, seized by the Manipur police, released. Regis Debray has written that once an insurgent group agrees to talk that is the beginning of the end to the insurgency. There have been no operations in Nagaland and Manipur since 1997, and that is a long five years. Though Muivah continues to make brave statements, I think he has begun to realize that he is not going to get much more. That is why a statement was made that there has to be a dialogue with the concerned states or districts where there is a Naga population. Muivah was probably hoping that as in the case of Mizoram, and Assam, the ruling group may step down and he could lead an over ground party to power in a Greater Nagaland. That is a faraway dream now, unless he has to return to the jungles, and I do not think that is what the Naga HoHo, or the Naga Baptist Church wants. He has to carefully slip out of the impasse with some skilful verbiage that will salvage an honourable settlement.

References

1. *Zelengam-The Kuki Nation.* P.S.Haokip. Published by the Kuki National Organisation. April 1, 998.
2. *Emergence of Nagaland.* Hokishe Sema. Vikas. 1982. p. 2.
3. *Origin and Culture of Nagas.* R.R.Shimray.Samsok Publications. New Delhi.
4. *My Experience in Manipur and Naga Hills.* James Johnstone. Sampson Low Marston and Company Ltd. London.

5. *The North Eastern Frontier of Bengal.* Alexander Mackenzie. 1884. Mittal Publications, Delhi. 1979.

6. *Nagaland.* Verrier Elwin. 1961. Shillong. Advisors Secretariat.

7. *The North East Frontier of Bengal.* Alexander Mackenzie. 1884. Mittal Publications Delhi. 1979. p. 55.

8. *Emergence of Nagaland.* Hokishe Sema. Vikas, 1986.

9. *Nagas Right to Self-Determination.* R.Vashum. Mittal Publications, 2000.

10. *Naga Insurgency.* M.Horam. Cosmo Publications. New Delhi. 1988. p.178.

11. Ibid., p. 179.

12. Ibid., pp. 179-180.

13. *The Land of Jade.* Bertil Lintner. White Orchid Press. Bangkok. 1992.

14. *The Pioneer.* October 2000. Deepak Sharma.

Blue Print for Counter-Insurgency in Manipur

Manipur has been seeing insurgency for the last 40 years, starting with the Federal Government of Nagaland [F.G.N.]. The insurgency of this group was initiated in the Naga hills district of Assam in 1956. It naturally spilled over into the four Naga dominated districts of Manipur. The base of the F.G.N. was in Ukhrul district, but Senapati and Tamenglong districts also provided solid support. The major contribution of cadres and leaders were from the Thangkhuls of Ukhrul, the Maos, Poumeis and Marams from Senapati district and the Zeliangs from Tamenglong district. Ukhrul district has a 140-kilometre unguarded border with Myanmar. To a depth of 20 kilometres from the border there are virtually no roads. The Yomadung and Angouching are the last north south ranges along the border. Across are the Somra tracts also populated by Thangkhuls. The slopes of the Yomadung and Angouching are thickly forested, and do not offer easy access for conventional troops. All along the border there is only one fair weather dirt road of Second World War vintage from Kamjong to the Chindwin valley. Terrain wise Ukhrul was a good district for the Naga underground army of the F.G.N. So were the districts of Senapati and Tamenglong, both thickly forested and with hardly any roads.

Later when the Shillong Accord was signed, peace returned to the four districts of Manipur. This peace was short-lived as Th. Muivah and Isaac Swu who were not a party to the Shillong accord, formed the Nationalist Socialist Council of Nagaland [N.S.C.N.] along with Kaphlang the Hemi Naga from north Myanmar. By 1980 the N.S.C.N. was operating in all the four Naga districts of Manipur. Later in 1988 the N.S.C.N. split in Myanmar and became two units, the N.S.C.N. [I.M.] led by Th. Muivah and Isaac Swu and the N.S.C.N. [K] led by Kaphlang. The N.S.C.N. [I.M.] did not lose much time in setting up their units in all the four Naga districts of Manipur.

Insurgency came to the valley districts of Manipur in the 1960s in the form of a shadowy Pan Mongoloid movement and the Revolutionary Government of Manipur. These groups preceded the creation of the United National Liberation Front of Manipur in November 1964 by Arambam Somerendra. The People's Revolutionary Party of Kangleipak [PREPAK] a chauvinist and revolutionary group was set up in October 1977 by R. K. Tulachandra. The People's Liberation Army [P.L.A.] was raised on September 25, 1978 by the late N. Biseswar. The reasons for the raising of these three organisations are not far to seek. The Meitei pseudo intellectuals never reconciled to the accession of Manipur in 1949 after nearly two years of India becoming independent. Manipur, an ancient kingdom with a 2000-year-old recorded history and a magnificent culture was made a part C state—a union territory. Then in 1962, Naga hills district of Assam was made a state, obviously a step to appease the secessionist F.G.N. Manipur continued to be a union territory for another ten years before being granted statehood. Manipuri, an ancient language spoken and written by all the Meiteis and tribals, was not included in the Eighth Schedule for years. The bureaucrats who came from Delhi and other states in 1949 were by and large not sympathetic to the Meiteis and the tribals. With a few exceptions, they did not win the confidence of the people of Manipur. The worst was the policy of the party in power in Delhi, of flooding the Northeast with funds and indirectly encouraging corruption, thinking it would make the people soft and end insurgency. It had just the opposite effect. It is not good to tamper with the self-respect of a people. A coterie of contractors, all followers of the party in power in Delhi was created which came to be called the Delhi Durbar who bagged most of the contracts in the Northeastern states. Ninety-five per cent of the development funds, which came from Delhi, were taken back to Delhi by this infamous band of contractors. Hundreds of kilometres of roads were built on paper and even annually maintained on paper. Foodgrains from the public distribution system were siphoned off wholesale into the black market. The politicians and bureaucrats of Manipur quickly adapted to this system.

The raising of the P.L.A., the U.N.L.F., and the PREPAK was a direct reaction to these factors. The P.L.A. raised in 1978 spread fast and was in full cry in the valley by 1979. A Meitei chauvinist group with its fierce leftist ideology and integrity attracted a cross section of educated youth. Many bright Meitei students from national universities abandoned their studies and joined the organisation. A series of dacoities and ambushes committed in 1978 and 1979 were attributed to the P.L.A. and the PREPAK. The object was to snatch arms from the police and the security forces and collect money for purchasing arms.

The heart of the business community is the Thengal and Paona bazaars, the home of the Marwaris and outside traders. They were key participants in the siphoning of essential goods into the black market. They naturally became a prime target of the P.L.A. and the PREPAK in extorting money. This extended to the coterie of outside contractors who had cornered the bigger contracts in the state. And from them to the corrupt politicians and bureaucrats was a natural step. The unholy nexus of the politician, bureaucrat and contractor in siphoning funds led to a fourth channel—the insurgent, who now claimed the biggest share at the point of the gun.

Terrain is a crucial factor in any insurgency. And in this the terrain of Manipur entirely favoured the insurgent. The hill ranges of Manipur are roughly north south. They peter off into the valley in the centre in a series of low hills. The hills are thickly forested and but for three national highways traversing them are bereft of roads. Of the five hill districts, Ukhrul to the east is exclusively Thangkhul Naga, with a few Kuki villages on the eastern border with Myanmar. N.H150 bisects Ukhrul, coming from Jessamie in the north and turning west enters the valley at Yanganpokpi. Border Roads have recently constructed a road from Shangshak near Ukhrul to Kasamkhullen in the south crossing into Chandel district connecting Tengnoupal. In the north Senapati district is bisected by N.H.39, coming from Kohima.There are two lateral roads to the west connecting Kangpokpi to Tamenglong and Maram to Paren and one to the east from Tadubi to Ukhrul. In Tamenglong a road links the district H.Q.s to Khongsang on N.H.53 coming from Imphal to Jiribam and to Silchar.From Churachandpur N.H. 150 was extended to Tipaimukh. This road has been abandoned for the last ten years. In Chandel district N.H.39

connects Palel to Moreh. The Tengnoupal New Samtal road constructed by the Border Roads has been abandoned. The interiors of Chandel and Churachandpur districts are the sanctuaries of the P.L.A., PREPAK, U.NL.F., K.C.P. and the myriad Kuki-Chin-Mizo underground groups and the hinterland from which they operate. The main base camps and training areas of the P.L.A. and the U.N.L.F. are in these two districts.

The P.L.A. and the U.N.L.F. initially had their hideouts in the Meithei villages in the valley, but established camps for training their cadres deep inside Chandel district and also inside Myanmar into which they crossed easily as the border was not policed. Initially weapons were purchased from the Myanmar army but a clandestine arms market gradually developed across the border of Chandel district. The break up of the Khmer Rogue in Cambodia and the later peace agreement between the Shan State and Myanmar released a whole lot of Russian and US army weapons into the arms market. In the 1970s when the P.L.A. and PREPAK were raised arms were not easily available. Their arsenal was built up by capturing arms from the police and para military forces and buying from the poorly paid Myanmarese soldiers deployed across the borders of India.

The army operated extensively against the P.L.A. in the early 1980s. In a series of swift operations they were able to capture the S.S. chief of the P.L.A., N.Biseswar and kill a number of top ranking leaders. The P.L.A. was halted in its tracks. Biseswar on his release took to politics, and became an M.L.A. The hard core of the P.L.A. though dormant was intact. Later after eliminating Biseswar, for changing tracks they regrouped and along with the N.S.C.N. and U.L.F.A.

sought help in arming and training its cadres with the Kachin Independent Army in northern Myanmar. All three groups got good training but not many arms. Except for a few Chinese M-22, the equivalent of the A.K.-47, they only got G-3 rifles and old weapons captured from the Myanmar army. In 1990, Bransen the K.I.O. leader withdrew support to the N.S.C.N., P.L.A. and U.L.F.A. and all three turned to Bangladesh for sanctuary. Here they got support beyond measure from the Bangladesh Government and the I.S.I. in the Pakistan embassy in Dacca. It was around this time that the Khmer Rogue broke up in Cambodia releasing a number of A.K.-47s,R.P.D.7.62 L.M.Gs and R.P.G.-7 rocket launchers into the clandestine arms market of South East Asia. The Pakistan I.S.I. seized this opportunity to sponsor the North Eastern insurgent groups. The first consignment of arms purchased in Thailand was landed in Cox's Bazaar in 1991, where a group of 240 N.S.C.N. cadres were waiting to receive them. It was carried overland via Bandarban, Parva, the eastern border of Mizoram, along the Tiddim road into Churachandpur district, then over the hills to Tamenglong and then into Paren subdivision of Nagaland. All the major insurgent groups linked with the N.S.C.N. got its weapons through this channel. In 1997 the drug lord Khun Sa surrendered to the Myanmarese Government. This led to the release of more arms to the clandestine arms market. Groups like the U.N.L.F., the K.C.P., and the different Kuki militant outfits found that they could buy arms from across the border from Chandel district

The other main valley group, the United National Liberation Front [U.N.L.F.] was founded by Arambam Somerendra in 1964 initially as a social organisation. It was the culmination of several movements like the Pan Mongoloid movement and the Revolutionary Nationalist Party, which raised the banner of independence in 1953. The U.N.L.F. took to arms only in the late 1980s. The self-styled chief of this group Rajkumar Meghen has royal lineage and was linked with the N.S.C.N. It is reported that he was in the know of the plans of Kaphlang to attack Th.Muivah and Isaac Swu and their followers in northern Myanmar and did not alert Muivah, as a result of which many of his followers were killed and Th. Muivah himself barely escaped with his life. Since then the N.S.C.N [I.M] cut off all links with the U.N.L.F. Rajkumar Meghen continues his close links with the N.S.C.N. [K].

By the 1990s some of the P.L.A. cadres left the group, came over ground and joined politics, and after the 2000 elections even became ministers. Today the P.L.A. and the U.N.L.F. maintain that they do not believe in the elections conducted by India. The smaller groups, particularly the myriad Kuki outfits each supported candidates of different parties who hired them. This included all the main national parties, except the Communist parties. They openly used arms to rig the elections both in 2000 and 2002.

The F.G.N. was the first to introduce extortion to Manipur. The N.S.C.N.[I.M] took over where they left off and systematised it to an annual house tax and ration tax. In addition they taxed all buses and trucks and contractors. At times their subordinate formations muscled in on development funds by coercing the Deputy Commissioners. The U.N.L.F. and P.L.A. at first took donations for their social activities, which gradually transformed into extortions. The target was of course the unholy trio of the politician, the bureaucrat and the businessman. It later spread to the salaried government servant. By the 1990s this had become institutionalised. Cashiers of different departments were directed to deduct percentages according to the ranks and pay to the organisation. They regularly taxed traders and businessmen. Tankers of petrol, diesel and kerosene oil were diverted from the big dealers and sold in the black market by all the major underground groups. Rice from the public distribution system was also diverted from all the dealers by these groups. A part was taken for supplying the underground camps. As a result, rice, kerosene, petrol and diesel were all sold in the black market. Against the quota of 5 litres per family per month of kerosene oil, most people were getting only one or two litres in Imphal, while in the interior towns and villages, there was no P.D.S supply at all. In the interiors of Chandel and Churachandpur districts, the P.L.A. and U.N.L.F. sold rice and kerosene at absurdly low rates to the villagers near their camps to get a Robin Hood image. In Imphal both the P.L.A. and the U.N.L.F. had well-oiled finance wings working. Their records were computerised and they had uptodate information of the receipt of development grants in the different departments. They had full knowledge of the bank accounts of all government officers, of doctors, engineers. Extortion demands were served accordingly. While there were standard deductions from all the government servants, doctors who also had good earnings from private practice got proportionate extortion demand notes. Officers dealing with development grants were forced to divert substantial sums to all the underground groups. Worse still Chief Engineers were forced to award contracts to cadres of the main insurgent groups at gunpoint. The members of the

Finance wing of the different groups had free access in all the government offices. Very often senior officials were summoned to chosen rendezvous on the outskirts of Imphal where they were forced at gunpoint to do the biddings of the groups. In the popular Government of 2000 the nexus between the P.L.A. and the U.N.L.F. with the politicians reached its peak.

All this could come about because of the trend set by politicians in siphoning off money in collusion with spineless bureaucrats. Money was collected from government servants for enhancing the pay scales. Large-scale diversion of development funds took place at the level of politicians and bureaucrats. It was only then that the insurgent groups intervened and started taking a major share in these deals. Most of the N.G.O.s in Manipur are run by politicians in the name of their hangers on. Grants obtained by them from the Centre for schemes like housing for the rural poor, watershed projects were largely siphoned off by these politicians. Only a trickle of about 5 per cent reached the people. In this background the development of this extensive extortion network is not a surprising development.

Of the five major valley underground groups the U.N.L.F. is the one whose ideology is by and large intact. The P.L.A. is better organised, but there are stories of P.L.A. cadres building big houses in Imphal. However, the senior leadership is well educated and has good organisational control. The lower cadres are mainly dropouts from school and college. The poor quality of education and the lack of jobs and entrepreneurial opportunities produce a pool of youth ready made for the insurgent groups. Of the five groups, the K.C.P. and K.Y.K.L exist mainly for extortion.

The P.L.A., U.N.L.F. and PREPAK have a loose collaboration and have worked out space allotments in the hinterland and operational areas. The K.Y.K.L. was formed by N. Oken when he walked out of the U.N.L.F. in 1990 and teamed up with splinter groups of the K.C.P. and the PREPAK. He established links with the N.S.C.N. [I.M.], the first and only penetration of the valley underground. K.Y.K.L. has a junior but extensive role in the extortion net in the valley and operates along with the N.S.C.N. [I.M.] cadres giving a share to them. The K.Y.K.L. had split into two factions in 1994 due to differences between Oken and Achou Toijamba, who linked up with the N.S.C.N. [K]. Recently in 2002, the two factions have patched up. Presumably the N.S.C.N. [I.M.] has won another round with Toijambas link with N.S.C.N. [K] severed.

Till the 1990s, the valley groups had operated only in the valley. They did use the secluded hills and jungles of Chandel district as their hinterland and had base camps and training areas there. This changed when the Kuki National Organisation [K.N.O] and the Kuki National Army [K.N.A.] were set up in 1992-93 in Tamu across the border town of Moreh.The Nagas and Kukis were ancient enemies The Kukis were the most enterprising of the Kuki-Chin Mizo group and had not restricted themselves to Churachandpur district were they had presumably first migrated. In their wanderings they occupied areas in Naga country in Ukhrul Tamenglong and Senapati districts and even occupied areas in the Naga Hills and North Cachar hills districts of Assam. The Kukis were used as a buffer against the Nagas both by the Meitei kings and the British. The K.N.O. and the K.N.A. were raised probably taking a leaf from history to again act as a buffer against the Nagas, now in the shape of the N.S.C.N. [I.M.]. Chandel district has a number of smaller tribes—Maring, Anal, Chothe, Kom, whom the Kukis claimed to be part of the Kuki-Chin-Mizo group, but with the rise of the F.G.N. and later the N.S.C.N., these tribes claimed that they were part of the Naga group. Whatever their origin, these small Naga tribes were numerically greater than the Kukis in Chandel district. This district is roughly bisected into two by the Pallel Moreh road. The eastern part adjoining Ukhrul is majority Naga. The area around Moreh is however dominated by Kukis. And Moreh is a smugglers town, with enormous profits to whoever controlled it. The N.S.C.N. [I.M.] had for long been eyeing it .The bait given to the Kukis in raising the K.N.O. and the K.N.A. was control of the rich spoils of smuggling of Moreh. Fierce clashes took place between the K.N.A. and the N.S.C.N. [I.M.] as they attacked each other's camps. Very soon they were attacking each other's villages, and both Naga and Kuki villages went up in flames. The N.S.C.N. [I.M.] were better trained, equipped and far more experienced. With years of fighting the Indian army they were better motivated. There ensued an ethnic cleansing of the Kukis in Ukhrul, Tamenglong and Senapati districts. The Kukis realising that they could not fight the battle on their own sought help from all their brother sub-tribes in Churachandpur district. Some of the sub-tribes responded positively, but the Paites, one of the larger and more prosperous of the Kuki-Chin-Mizo group refused to help and berated the Kukis for sticking their necks out unnecessarily. This angered the Kukis and they attacked the Paites in a fratricidal war. The Kuki-Paite clashes were bitterly fought and several Kuki and Paite villages were burnt. The Paites were not well armed and naturally took a

Chandel axis and the K.R.A. who operate in the Saikul valley. Earlier still another group had broken off from the K.N.O., the Kuki Liberation Organisation and the Kuki Liberation Army—the K.L.O. and the K.L.A.

This then is the unhappy state of affairs in Manipur. Can something be done to restore normalcy? A very determined effort will be required to stabilise the politics and administration of the state. The effort has to be a civil-military coordinated manoeuvre. The central government has always had a standard reaction to any insurgent situation—send a couple of battalions of central para military forces [C.P.M.F.] If very severe send in the army. Not in any insurgent situation have we analysed the causes of why an insurgent situation has developed, of why a group of people have taken to arms and is fighting the state. In Bihar when the Ranbir Sena had massacred thirty odd Scheduled Caste sympathisers of the M.C.C., a series of meetings were held in the Home Ministry and several battalions of C.P.M.F. were sent to Bihar. After some time when the situation was reviewed it was found that the forces sent were deployed to hunt for the M.C.C. and not for the Ranbir Sena. No one talked of the unlawful and unequal distribution of land and the denial of land to peasants because of their caste.

In any insurgent situation the causes must be first dispassionately analysed. This must be left to professional economists, sociologists, judges, professional police officers and professional administrators. The emphasis on professionals, qualifying police officers and administrators should be specially noted. In the last 30 odd years, the concept of committed bureaucracy has become deep rooted. It is of no use leaving judging of an insurgent situation to a police officer or administrator who is aligned to any political party and has earned his promotions by patronage.

Once this has been done a blue print for counter-insurgency should be drawn up. The effort has to be a combined civil and military effort with the civil leading all the way. This has to be clearly emphasised. There should be no question of the armed forces ever having the leadership in an insurgent situation. Heavy deployment of army or paramilitary forces is bound to cause excesses. This is unavoidable. And when this happens, without redressing the conditions of the population, which has in the first place led to the resort to arms by a section of the population, they are bound to get further alienated. It is imperative therefore that the civil effort should be supported by the military effort.

The first step in the kind of situation we are faced with in Manipur, where there is an undercurrent of secession, rampant corruption led by the politicians and tamely abetted by the bureaucrats and a complete failure by the state to protect the few upright government servants, is to list the local civil, judicial and police officers and identify the few who have not been tainted by chauvinism and corruption and, who if protected, are likely to stand up against intimidation. The second step is to post these officials in all crucial posts. The first preference should be for local officers. Where reliable local officers are not available, specially selected outside officers should be brought and posted. The third step is to ensure that reliable judicial officers are posted. This is a sphere that is invariably neglected, after the 1973 amendment of the Cr.P.C., separating the prosecution from the investigation. The police now forget the case after the charge sheet is filed. Every hearing should be followed to ensure that the underground is not taking advantage of the police not following the case to get their cadres released.

The judicial officers posted should be equally strict to the prosecution and to the defence, in fact more so to the prosecution. In every insurgency the judiciary is always used by the underground, mainly because the judiciary is always local, except for the Chief Justice. Also the judiciary does not get the kind of guards and escorts that the executive gets. There is no reason why the Judges from the sessions upto the High Court cannot be from outside. Their security should be more stringent than of the field officers. The judge who sentenced Maqbool Bhatt to death, was not protected, and he was shot later. After this no judge would have dared to sentence any insurgent to imprisonment, let alone death.

Special attention should be paid to bring up the police. The Manipur Rifles was a very fine force, which has degenerated because of very poor officering, and lack of finance resulting in the riflemen being forced to buy their own uniforms, Pay is never regular, as a result of which, the men are forced to borrow from the unit Bania canteen. A soldier who lives like this loses his self-respect, and cannot be expected to fight. The first step to be taken is to see that the ration of the riflemen is equated to that of the C.P.M.F. to ensure that he is paid in time, equipped well, and trained rigorously. The command of the battalions should be given to officers of the C.P.M.F. The civil police must immediately be reorganised and strengthened. Some of the districts have only about 200 personnel, no reserve lines, miserable barracks, which have not been repaired for years. All sub-inspectors and above should be put through in service courses in investigation, interrogation and intelligence trade craft.

There are pitfalls into which the police can easily fall when involved in counter insurgency operations. Fortunately we have examples at close hand. In Punjab, we saw the police picking, up innocent boys saying they were terrorists, and releasing them after taking money. This happened in Kashmir too. In Assam, Hiteswar Saikia, the then Chief Minister created a mafia after getting known U.L.F.A. criminals, who had murder cases pending against them, and forming them into mafia gangs, extorting money from coal transporters. The surrendered U.L.F.A. boys were allowed to keep their weapons and operate as gangs under unofficial patronage. In all these cases, who were the victims? The victims were the very people who were to be won over to the government's side, and who were to be weaned away from the insurgents. All you got was an indignant populace, who got further alienated and a police force who had become terrorists themselves. In Manipur, civil policemen and officers were selected and trained as commandos. They did a commendable job initially, but soon deteriorated to a state terrorist force, because of faulty leadership. They began extorting money from the business community, picking a leaf out of the insurgent's book. What was the consequence on the hapless public? Here were five to six underground groups extorting money from the traders, and here was a special wing of the police force, set up to arrest the under ground, who also demanded their share of extortions. Now to whom was the hapless public to turn to? These are lessons before us and that is why it is imperative that in all such situations the leadership of the police force should be very carefully chosen.

The same rules apply to the civil administration. We have seen the way politicians and bureaucrats siphoned away development funds, diverted essential commodities to the black market, and built roads on paper. It is very necessary to screen all the civil servants in such a situation and list out the personnel who are honest and not tainted with underground sympathies. One of the most important steps to be undertaken is to ensure that all essential commodities of the P.D.S. are made available to the public right to the remotest villages at the correct prices. This is not too difficult a task as can be seen by the experiment below. When President's rule was declared in June 2001, kerosene oil was being sold at Rs. 25 to Rs. 30 in Imphal and consumers were getting just one or two litres per month. The condition was much worse in the districts and in the remote villages the P.D.S. was defunct. Of the 100 odd tankers of petrol, diesel and kerosene oil, coming to Imphal weekly, the thirty odd tankers of kerosene oil would not even report at the I.O.C. depot, but would drive to the dealers, who would divert most of them to the black market. The huge storage reservoirs of the I.O.C. depot were empty for many months. The main valley underground groups of course had their share in this diversion. The P.L.A., U.N.L.F., PREPAK and others regularly took two to three tankers of kerosene oil and sold them in the black market. The rest of the black marketing was done by the traders. The C.R.P.F. was deployed in the I.O.C. depot and movement of unauthorised personnel strictly restricted. The members of the finance wing of the underground groups found that they had no access to the depot. All tankers coming from Dimapur were stopped at Mao on the Manipur border, the challans taken from them and escorted to Imphal by the Manipur Rifles. In Imphal, they were parked in the Manipur Rifles campus for the night and escorted to the depot in groups of ten tankers.

There storage tanks were filled for the first time in several months. From the depot kerosene oil tankers were escorted to the district dealers by the Manipur Rifles. In Imphal, 50 per cent of the dealers quota was directed to be sold in mobile sale directly by the dealer to the public on ration cards—ten litres per family at Rs. 8 per litre. This was supervised. Long queues of women and children were a familiar sight after that all getting kerosene oil at the correct price. There were some attempts by the underground to disrupt the sale. But no one had the courage to buck the public when the government was doing a correct job. Within a month the black market price of kerosene oil had come down to Rs. 11 to Rs.12 in the city. It was reliably learnt that one or two underground groups diverted two to three tankers of kerosene oil from some of the dealers, but sheepishly returned them, as they could not find any buyers. In the districts where the Deputy Commissioners were honest, they were able to get kerosene oil to the interior villages by escorting the tankers, or carrying the kerosene oil in drums. Very effectively both the traders and the underground were defeated. Not giving up the fight, one of the underground groups served a notice on the I.O.C. depot to pay Rs. 10 lakhs to them .The staff sensibly reported this to the police. The staff quarters were adjacent to the storage depot and was guarded by the C.R.P.F. Several telephone calls were made to the I.O.C. manager. He was told not to respond to the calls and to confine himself to his quarters after work. The C.R.P.F. was directed to enhance their vigil and always escort the manager and his staff. The I.O.C. Mangement was contacted and requested to post personnel for two months at a time to the depot at Imphal. They cooperated. There was one attempt to kidnap the manager when he crossed from one depot to the other, but he was escorted by two C.R.P.F. guards who were alert, and the group gave up the attempt even before they could get started. After several more futile calls, the group gave up the attempt. Constant monitoring and visits by senior officers, thwarted the attempt of the underground in this case.

It is very necessary to ensure that all civil police and judicial officers are guarded both at office and in their residences. For this the Home Ministry must set apart 2 to 3 battalions of C.R.P.F. and direct the state police to see that they guard the offices, residences and escort all these officials. In the case of engineers, forest officers, and officers of development departments, all of them should be escorted to their work sites. The counter-insurgency grid must therefore visualise a sizeable force. The main area for extortions is of course Imphal. Extensive coverage of the city is absolutely necessary. Continual cordon and search operations are also unavoidable. It must be ensured that all such operations are done in the presence of magistrates. While all this is done it must always be ensured that the civil administration has been cleaned up and the public is getting essential commodities at correct prices, does not have to pay to get recruited or promoted. If the people feel that the government is responsible they will tolerate the inconvenience and indignity of cordon and searches. But if it is the same corrupt government then they will only be further alienated. One way to ensure this is to see that officers at the highest levels are accessible to the public.

One sphere on which the state has done well is that of agriculture. In the valley today with just about 20 per cent double cropping the valley produces enough rice to feed 80 per cent of the population of the whole state. This can easily be improved by concentrating on minor irrigation schemes, and double cropping brought upto 80 per cent. Within two to three years Manipur can be made a surplus state in rice. In the hills there is tremendous scope for horticulture, piggery, fisheries, poultry farming, and dairy farming. It will also be necessary to take up conversion of slash and burn agriculture to terrace farming. A number of roads should be constructed to link the interiors with the market towns. The beautiful Khoupum valley produces excellent oranges, which go a-begging, as the road to Bishnupur has been abandoned. The construction of roads into the interior should be coordinated with the setting up of the counter-insurgency grid in the hills.

The main concentration of deployment in the hills should be in the districts of Chandel and Churachandpur, the hinterland of the main valley groups. A careful study will show that most of the tracks in the hills are along the ridge lines or along the river valleys. It is imperative therefore to deploy along all the ridge lines in these two districts. Extensive use of helicopters for logistics is unavoidable. Once this is done, the groups will have no choice but to slip into Myanmar. Once this happens and the ridgelines and valleys in these two districts are held, it will be necessary to deploy the B.S.F. on the Arunachal Pradesh, Nagaland, Manipur and Mizoram international border with Myanmar. This is going to be expensive, but necessary.

In the hills the C.I. operations must first concentrate on the rebel Kuki groups, like the U.K.L.F., the K.R.A. and the Z.R.A. who have links with the N.S.C.N. [I.M.]. There is always the tendency to use one group against the other. This has been done in Kashmir, in Assam, using the S.U.L.F.A. against the U.L.F.A., and in Manipur, using groups like the Z.R.A. against the P.L.A. This kind of strategy should never be resorted to.. It is immoral and unethical to arm any group or allow it to keep its arms. There should be no question of any one having unlicensed arms. The aim of the C.I. operations should be to see that not a single unlicensed arm remains with any one. There should be no question of any group feeling insecure, and buying arms for their security. The N.S.C.N. [I.M.] should not be allowed to keep any arms in Manipur. This should be strictly enforced. This group has been pampered beyond measure. After the smaller groups are de fanged, the major valley groups should be taken on. In the hills, particularly in Chandel and Churachandpur, the ridge lines should be occupied and the main camps taken on in the river valleys. While these operations are being conducted the valley areas should be carefully cordoned so that the groups do not filter back. This will force the groups to go to Myanmar, and then to Bangladesh. The deployment of B.S.F. on the borders should now be taken up. Simultaneously, The Border Roads should take up extensive construction of roads on the borders. As and when the interior areas are cleared the civil effort should follow on the heels of the armed forces. The armed forces deployment should continue till the roads are constructed, water supply schemes implemented, electricity conductors and substations set up, health centres opened, horticultural and other schemes taken up. As all this is being done the government should slowly privatise. There are many spheres where the government should disengage, like collection of power tariff, irrigation, cess, etc. The government can also disengage in the field of education and health care. This should be given increasingly to the missionary institutions.

During the C.I. operations magistrates and police should be associated with all cordon and search operations. Suspects picked up by the armed forces should be handed over to joint interrogation centres immediately. All cadres from whom weapons are recovered should be detained, under the N.S.A. and their trials under the Arms Act or other special acts should be closely monitored. Special courts should be set up for this. Whenever there are interim stay orders granted the higher courts must be appealed to, and the stays vacated. Special day-to-day hearings should be carried out in all-important cases.

It must be borne in mind that our powerful neighbour China is not far from Manipur and the Northeast. All the major insurgent groups in the Northeast have at one time or the other met the Chinese government and got arms from them. Today the Myanmar government has become heavily dependent on them. The Myanmar army is equipped with Chinese arms. It is reliably learnt that arms from the Chinese ordnance factories are trickling into the clandestine arms market in Myanmar. Recently the Myanmar special unit NA-SA-KA is reported to have arrested 36 cadres of the valley insurgents from Kalemyo and seized 1600 weapons from them. It is learnt that the cadres have been released after payment of heavy fines. The weapons have been kept by the Myanmar army. All the weapons were reported to be of Chinese origin. The question is, were the weapons released to the arms market by design or by accident.

We must clearly understand that Manipur is geographically, ethnically and linguistically South East Asian. We have neglected this beautiful land and beautiful people too long. Instead of nurturing this frontier state, we have allowed its politics and administration to degenerate. Despite all this, the people are remarkably patient. When one visits remote villages with an inaccessible dirt road, no water supply, no electricity, no primary health centre, and a dilapidated primary or middle school without any teachers, one is impressed by the warmth of the welcome of the people, for just deigning to visit their village. One feels ashamed. The state is so small, the population so limited, it is not difficult to bring it up. All that one requires is the will.

References

1. Robert Thompson. *Defeating Communist Insurgency.*
2. Sir James Johnstone. My *Experiences in Naga Hills and Manipur.*
3. R. Constantine. *Manipur, Maid of the Mountains.*
4. Vedaja Sanjenbam. *Manipur, Geography and Regional Development.*

Acknowledgements

I am deeply grateful to K.E.Priyamvada for editing all the five essays and initiating me into the mysteries of the computer.

Index

Achik National Volunteer Council (A.N.V.C.) 98, 132, 137
Adam Sena, 106
Advisory Committee of aboriginal trihes of Nagas, 121
Afghan Mujahideen camp, Peshawar
  ULFA Cadres training, 54-57, 135
Agotito Hill, 128
Al Qaida, 85, 110
Ali, Dodar, 128
All Assam Gana Sangram Parishad, 23-24, 28, 39
All Assam Students Union (A.A.S.U.), 21-27, 41-42, 57, 133
All Boro Students Unions (A.B.S.U.), 59-60
All Tripura Tiger Force (A.T.T.F.), 80, 101-102
Amir, Naib, 107
Angami, T.N., 123
Angami, Mehiasiu, 129
Angami, Mowu, 129
Armed Forcets Special Powers Act, 113
Assam
  agricultural production 64-65
  black market, 68
  economic growth rate, 14
  ethnic classes, 33,105
  Centres neglect y, 63-64
  drop out percentage, 66
  revamnping of education system, 70
  riots, 53
  unemployed numbers, 14-15
Assam Accord
  51, 130, 150
Assam election of 1983, 39, 49, 51
  A.P.L.A. operates on C.R.P.F., 39-40
  Sub-inspector Kill of episode,39-40
Assam-Cachar and Karimganj District Border with Bangladesh, 99-100
Assam-Dhuhri District Border stretch of, 96-97
Assam Disturbed Areas Act, 113, 123
Assam Jatiyati badi Yuba Chatra Parishad (A.J.Y.C.P), 23, 25
Assam Peoples Liberation Army (A.P.L.A.), 14, 28, 39-40
Assam Rifles, 113
Asomiya Samrakhini Sabha, 110
Assan Sahitya Sabha, 23
Assamiya Basha Unnati

Sadhani Sabha (1888), 9
Aung San Su Kyi's League for Democracy, 78
Bank robbery, 131-132
Bangladesh
creation 7,10,27,76
lebensraum question in, 104-105
Bangladesh Directorate of Forces Intellogence (D.G.F.I.) 55-56, 101-107, 110-111, 135-137, 150
Bangladesh Islamic Manch, 111
Bangladeshi Refugees, 7-11, 14-16, 74,95,104
Bangladesh Rifles, 80
Bangladesh Taliban, 109-110
Bargohain, Badreswar, 40
Bargohain, Bhim Kanta, 40
Baruah, Golap, 40-41, 53-55
Baruah, Paresh, 40-41, 46-47, 54,62
Bengali babu
Competition between Assamiya middle class and, 8-9
Bhatt, Maqbool, 168
Bhattacharya, Kamala Kanta, 9
Biswas, Charu, 81
Biseswar, N., 154,157
Boro Peoples Action Committee (BPAC), 59-60
Boro Security Force (Bd.S.F), 59-61 see N.D.F.B.
Bhutan
ABSU and BPAC
relations with 60
weapons twon, 69
Bora, Jnananath, 10
Border Out Post (B.O.P.) 73, 86-87, 90, 96-98, 103, 112
Border Security Force (BSF), 78, 80, 83, 86, 89, 93-94, 100-102, 122-136, 145-146, 173
Border Smuggling Force, 86
Bordoloi, Gopinath, 11
Brahmaputra Valley, 1, 4, 9, 21-22, 28, 41, 65, 117
Bronsen,134
British Cabinet Mission, 121
Bru National Liberation Front (B.N.L.F.),144
Buams
worst condition of, 84
Buddhist temples
burning of, 77
Bukhtiyar, Mohammad Ibn, 3
Bureaucracy
Committed, 30, 166 coterie of, 70
Businessmen
extortion of money, 63
Butler, John, 6
Cease Fire Monitoring Group, 143-145
Census Report of Assam of 1931, 9-10
C.R.P.F., 33, 36-39, 43, 59, 170-

172
Chakma, Sneha Kumar, 81
Chakmas
Bangladesh Muslims attack, 78
Citizenship demand, 74
death knell for, 81
discrimination, 74
Chakmas displacement of, 76
district Council, 74
lack of health, education etc, 74
migration of, 101
population 73-74, 84
problems, 73-74
second class citizens treatment, 74,149
temples destruction, 79
women rape, 80
worst conditions of, 78
Chetia, S.S.Lt., 45
Chief Election Commissioner of India, 23-24
China
arms puchase from 46,62, 127,131,134,146-147,158,175
Chindwin valley, 153
Chins of Burma, 120
Chittagong of Hill Tracts (CHT), 99, 120, 137, 142
CHT
autonomous district creation, 75
CHT
area, 74-75
Bangladesh Muslims in, 79
British Act of 1900,75
British annexation, 75
Buddhist and Christian percentage,75
Chakmas youth hoisting Indian Tri Colour at Rengamati, 75
ethnic groups, 75
insurgency, 77
insurgent groups, 80
Marmas hoisting the Burmese flage at Bandarhan, 75
Pak lowering down the Indian tri colour at gunpoint, 75
Radcliffie decison, 75,81
Skirmishes between Bangladesh army and Shanti Bahini, 77
Christian group of Boros, Udalguri, 59
Coal and fish mafia disbandment of 69
role, 58-60
Constitution of India, 27, 149
Corruption, 13,67, 13,67
C.P.M.F.- Couple of Battalions of Central Para Military, 166,169
Crown Colony
Nagas opposition, 120
Dacoity, 154
Debray, Regis, 151
Defence Institute of

Bangladesh, 83
Democratic Party, 127
Development money
politicians diverting of, 64-65
Dewan, Maniram
hanging of, 6
Dhansiri Project
successful, 64-65
Dima Halem
Daoga (D.H.D.), 132,139
East India Company, 4-5,100
Election of 1952 and 1957
N.N.C. boycott of, 123, 127
Emergency (1975), 30-31
Extortion, 41,44-45,47-78,
59,61-63,117,131,132,
139-144,159-160
Fakruddin, Maulana
Md, 107
Federal Government of
Nagaland (F.G.N.)
setting up of, 123,
127-131,153
Foreigners' Agitation
Fuji, Abu, 110
Gogoi, Pradeep, 40
Gogoi, Saurabh, 58
Gohain, Chakra, 58
Golden Bird operation, 142
Government of India
Act of, 1919, 118
Government of peoples
Republic of Nagaland
(G.P.R.N.), 131
Greater Nagaland, 151
Guha, 9
Guerrilla warfare, 59
Hafiz, Maulana, 106
Hajo - Pua Mecca
or Small Macca, 4
Haloi, 45
Hmar People's Convention
Democratic (H.P.C.D.)
Mizoram underground
group, 132, 138, 165
Haque, Azizul, 108
Harkat-ul-Ansar
(H.U.A.), 95,99
Harkat-ul-Jihad-e-Islam
(H.U.J.I.), 85,
95,99,106,109-110
Harkat-ul-Mujahideem
(H.U.M.), 85,95,106-109
Hasina, Sheikh,78-79
Harshavardhan, 3
Hemi Naga, 131
Heroin
hot issue, 87
Hieuen Tsang, 3
Huire, Zashi, 130
Hussaini, Mohammed
Fasiullah alias
Hamid Mohammed, 106
Hynniewtrep Achik
Liberation Council (H.A.L.C.)
split of, 137
Hynniewtrep National
Liberation Council

(H.N.L.C.), 98,132,137
Hydari, Sir Akbar, 122
Indira-Mujib Pact, 27
Indian Army, 83,123,142
Indian Citizenship Act, 27
Indian Independence Act, 81
Infiltrators, 86,87
Irrigation Projects of Assam
doldrums, 64-70
Insurgency in Kashmir
Pak plan,86-87
International border (I.B.)
fencing and lightning,87
policing, 85-86
Islamic Chatra Shibir,109
Islamic Liberation Army
of Assam (I.L.A.A.)106
Jadonang,119
Jamaat-e-Islam,108
Jamiat-e-Ulema-e-
Islam(J.U.M.),85
Jana Samhiti Samiti
(J.S.S.),76-78
Jasokie, J.B.,123
Jatiya Mahasabha
declaration of indepen-
dent Assam,10
Jenkins, Captain,118
Johnstone, James,116
Jumma
atrocities,77
autonomous demand,76
CHT-Bangladesh
settling,76
Bangladesh peace treaty
78-79
conversion to Islam,77
counter-insurgents
operations,77
maltreatment,79
massacre,77-78
mistake of negotiation
with Sheikh Hasina,80
Mukti Bahini rampage
against,76
Pak's discrimination
refugees,79
Kachin Independent
Organisation (K.I.O.),
46,133-134
Kamtapur Liberation
Organization (K.L.O.),61
Kanglei Yawol Kanna
Lup (K.Y.K.L.), 140,143,
161-162
K.Y.K.L.(O).a Meithei
insurgent group, 132
Kaphlang, 131,154
Karbi Anglong
case of,149
Kargil war
U.L.F.A. support
Pakistan, 63
Karim, Fazle,110
Karnaphuli river, Kaptai
dam construction,74,76
Khader, Abdul,108
Khalistan groups,87
Khan, Sadiq,104
Khasi Insurgent

groups,98
Khmer Rogue in Cambodia
break up of 157-158
Kidnapping,43-44,51-52,129,138-139,144,151
Kitson, Sir Frank,59
Kuki-Chin-Mizo groups,141,157,162-163
Kuki National Army,(K.N.A.),141,162-166
K.N.F. (Presidential),140
K.N.F.(M.C.),140
Kuki National Organization (K.N.O.),140,162-165
Kuki Revolutionary Army (K.R.A.),132,140,141,143,173
Lachit Sena,13
Lashkar-e-Taiba (L.E.T.)95
Larma, M.N.,76
Lindh, John Walker,109
Lintner, Bertil,46,133
McCabe, R.B.,149
Mallick, B.N.19
Manipur Insurgency
beginning of, 153
dacoities and ambushes,154
extortion of money, 159 160
Insurgents groups,140,154-175
N.S.C.N(IM) foothold in,139-140
Manipur Rifles, 147,168 171
M.C.C.,166
Marwaris,7-8,12-13,44-45,63,100,138,155
Master, Akram,107
Medom, Biseto,130
Meghalaya border,97-98
Meghen, Raj Kumar,159
Mehta, ViJalie,130
Migration wave,6-10
Mizoram Border with Bangladesh,
account of,103-104
Mizo Hills, 73-74
Mizo Insurgency (1966)
beginning of,138
Mizo National Front (M.N.F.),132
Mogs
plight of,84
Mohanta, Hirak Jyoti,43
Mohanta, Kishore,58
Moorish,108
Mountbatten, Lord,121
Muivah, Thuingaleng, 129-131,134-135,150-151,153,159
Mukherjee, Bijon,81
Mukti Bahini,76
Mullan, C.S.,10,16
Muslim United Liberation Front of Assam(M.U.L.F.A.),105

Muslim United Liberation Tigers of Assam (M.U.L.T.A.),106,111
Muslim Volunteer Force (M.V.F.),106
Mushmudeem, Mohammad,107
M.V.Meeca,109-110
Myanmar
  arms market,175
  bordering of,107-108
Myanmarese Army,46,77
Naga Accord (1975),130-131
Naga Army, 123,131
Naga Club (1918),120
Nagaland Election,127,140
Naga Hills,116-117,121,124-125,127
Naga Hills District Council, 121
Naga Hills District of Assam, 124
Naga Hills District Samagooting (Chumukdima)l18,123
Naga HoHo,151
Naga Home Guard or Naga Underground Army,123
Naga Insurgency
  background of,113,150
  begining of 138
  causes, 113,119
  different insurgent groups role,115
  ethnic clashes,140
  explosives,127
  Cease-Fire Agreement,128-129,143-145,147-148,153-154
  Government mistakes,124-127
  Kuki division,113
  literature,113
  Meitheis history,116,117
  peace missions,128-129
  Regulation of 1880
  skirmishes between underground naga army and Jaidinliu,119-120
  surrender before BSF,136-137
  traditional enmity between Kuki-Chin Mizo group,131
  violence,127
  weaponse,135-137
Naga National Council 1946(N.N.C.),121-124
Naga National Independence ceremony, boycott of,122
Nagaland National Organization (N.N.O.),127,131,150
Naga Peace Council (1974),130

Naga People's convention, 1957, Kohima(N.P.C.), 124
Naga village 115-117,126,148
National Democratic Front of Boroland,131
National Socialist Council of Nagaland (N.S.C.N.),41,46,98,131,139 150,154,157-159
split of,133-134
NS.C.N.(M),55-56,80,101,134,154,159, 164-165,173-174
ambushes on security forces,132
Aizawl Camp,104
bank robheries,132
Bangladesh link,103
extortion network of,142
government dialogue with,143,151
indian army killing(103)
money sharing,138
moving along border of Mizoram,56
nexus between the party in power,104
offices of,133
operations,137
Pak I.S.I. arranging weapons,56
scope for extention,138
surrender before the BSF,56,136-137,145-146
weapons from Thailand,56,57
N.S.C.N.(K),134,154,159.162
Nagaland State(1963)
inauguration of,124
National Democratic Front of Bodoland(N.D.F.B.),56,98, 137,142
National Liberation Front of Tripura(N.L.F.T.),80,101,132
National Register of Citizens,1951,25
N.S.A.,175
Naxalite Movement,13-14
Negi, Daulat Singh,58
Nehru, Jawaharlal,10-12,81,121
Nepalese immigration into Bhutan,60
North Cachar Hills,127,132,138
Northeastern Council (N.E.C.),67,68
Oil refinery, 11-12
agitation,13
blowing up of, 135
U.L.F.A. sabotage plan,54
OP.Bajrang,31,45-46,49,55
OP Rhino,55

Pak infiltration post (P.I.P.),19
Pakistan inter-services intelligence(I.S.J.),54,56, 86-87,105-107,127,134-135,137,150
Pal,. Surendra
Killing of,44-45
Pan Mongoloid Movement,154,159
Parbattya Chattogram Jana Samiti,81
Paresh,Barua,135
Parva,137
Patel, Sardar,11,81
Pemberton,118
Peoples Liberation Army of Manipur (P.L.A),41,46,100,131,133-134,137,154-161,164,170,174
P.L.A. Bangladesh,56,59
Peoples Revolutionary Party of Kangleipak (PREPAK),154-156,157,165,170
Peoples United Liberation Front (P.U.L.F.),106
Phizo, A.Z.,122-123,127,131
Phukan, Rebati,47,50
Phukan, Suddartha,54
Politicians
coterie of,70
diversion of development funds,64-65
patronage to U.L.F.A.,63
Presidents Rule in Assam,20,48
Primary School(Assam)
burning episode,29-30
P.D.S.
clean up of,68-69,170
Punjab
terrorist groups,86
Punjab Border
fencing and lightning,87
Radcliffe,75,81,91
Rajasthan Border
fencing and lightning,87-88
Raj Kumar, Aurobinda,40,54
Ramyo,Z,129
Ranbir Sena,166
Rape,77,80,84
Refugee camps,89
Rehman, Sheikh Mujibar,27,76,83-84
Rehman, Ziaur,83-84
Reid, Sir Roberty,120
Religious institutions
destruction of, 77
Rice smuggling,12-13
Riverine border,112
Revolutionary Government of Nagaland

(R.G.N.),129
Revolutionary Nationalist
Party, Manipur,159
Rohingyas
driving out by
Myanmar,78
Rohingyas refugees,108
Rohingya Solidarity
Organization,
(R.S.O.),108,109
Roychoudhary,10
Saikia, Hiteswar,50-51
Sakhrie,T.,123
Salim, Quari
Sangram Parishad,12,21
Sarkar, Manik,145
Sarma, Joynath,21
Scott, David,5
Security Problem,83-84
Security Zone,111
Sema, Hokishe,129-130
Sema, Kaito,127,129
Sema, Scatu Swu,129
Shanti Bahini,76-78
Shillong Accord,153-154
Shimray, Anthony,149
Simon Commission,120
Singh, Gambhir,5
Smuggling,87
Somerendra,
Arambam,154,158
South East Asia Insurgencies,125,149-150
Special Court,49
Sukapha, Shan Prince,4
Superintendent's wife of
Assam episode,42-43
S.U.L.F.A., 59,69,174
Swu, Isaac,130-
131,134,150-151
Tagore, Rabindranath,84
Tea Gardens,5-7,16
Thailand
weapons purchase from,
55-57,61,101,103,135-
137,142
Thompson Sir Robert,28-
125-126
Treaty of
Yandaboo(1826),5,149
Tripura insurgency,100-
101
Tulachandra, P.K.,154
Unemployed youth of
Assam of, 63
United Kuki Liberation
Front
(U.K.L.F.),132,143,165
United Liberation Front
of Assam (U.L.F.A.),
25,80,96,98,131-
134,137,142-143,159,169
Army Capture of
weapons,55
Army operation,4 7-5
Army withdrawal,52
Bangladesh names and
passport to cadres,135

Bangladesh visit,53-54
Pak visit,53-54
Camps at Bhutan,61
China visit,62
Civil and police killings,47
Communication network,62
corruption story,62-63
counter-insurgency operation,52
Digboi headquarter,47
distribution of pamphelts,53
erosion in support,58
extortion of money,41,43,62-63
fight with Myammar Army,46
flow of money,47
getting bank accounts from the bank,41
government employees support,47
kidnapping of officials,43-45,51-52
K.I.A. training,46-47
leaders arrest,49,53
leaders release demand,51-52
leader surrender,50
link with A.A.S.U.,41-43,48
link with the Bhutanese government,61-62
links with K.L.O.,62
mentors,40-41
network,41
operation of,41
plea for dialogue,69
police and civil service soft attitude,42
police raid,44
political patronage,59,63
rural and urban people support,48
Russian mining engineer killing,51
strength of,61-62
Surendra Pal killing 44-45
SP's wife story,42-43
Tibet visit,62
training in N.S.C.N. camp,46
unemployed youth continuing market for,63
weapons purchase,46
weapons training,135
United Muslim Liberation Front of Assam(U.M.L.F.),106
United National Liberation Front (UNLF),100-102,140,154-155,157-161,164-170,174-175
United Nation,78
U.N.H.C.R.,78

United Peoples Democratic Solidarity(U.P.D.S.),132-139
Unlawful Activities Act,130
Vincent,Lt,116
Wakhar,Md.Javed,106
Wavell,Lord,16
West Bengal Border,88-96
Yallay, Kevi,130
Zeliangrong Nagas,
Zhia Bharali,121-122
Zia, Pak President,76
Zia, Khaleda,79
Zomi Reunification Army(Z.R.A.),132-141,164,173-174
Z.R.O,141,143

UBS|330697|45